WHY KEEP SUNDAY SPECIAL

by

Christopher Townsend

and

Michael Schluter

D1455711

Foreword

by

Sir Norman Anderson

Jubilee Centre Publications Ltd.
114, Barton Road, Cambridge CB3 9LH, England

First Edition July 1985
Second Edition October 1985

ISBN 0 948476 00 1

Scripture quotations in this publication are from the Holy Bible, New International Version. Copyright 1973, 1978, International Bible Society. Quotations from Cmnd. 9376 'Report on the Committee of Inquiry into Proposals to Amend the Shops Acts' (Chairman, Mr. Robin Auld, QC) and from *Hansard* are reproduced with the permission of the Controller of Her Majesty's Stationery Office.

Typeset and printed by Elitian Ltd., 112 Mill Road, Cambridge CB1 2BD.
Published by Jubilee Centre Publications Ltd., 114 Barton Road, Cambridge CB3 9LH, England.

CONTENTS

FOREWORD

I welcome, and commend to the public at large, this succinct statement on a very controversial subject of great common concern. I, for one, know no other summary which is so comprehensive, balanced and persuasive.

This booklet sets out to alert those who profess and call themselves Christians to the value of keeping Sunday as a day set especially apart for public worship, personal relaxation and the enjoyment of their families and friends. But it does not stop here, for it goes on to explain why they should do all they can to convince others that this is salutary for society as a whole. Essentially positive rather than negative in its approach, it also provides substantial answers to the arguments - economic, social, legal and ideological - of those who range themselves on the other side in the debate on Sunday trading.

The present law on this subject certainly needs rationalisation, and probably partial relaxation. But to remove all legal control would be 'putting the clock back' on the wisdom and practice of long centuries in favour of a doctrinaire reliance on 'market forces'. Some would, no doubt, benefit financially; but society as a whole would suffer, and especially those who most need protection.

The authors rightly emphasise the essential difference between the rigid Old Testament law of the Sabbath, as a basic sign of God's covenant with Israel, and the special nature that most Christians attach to Sunday. In this the authors part company with the stridency of a Victorian insistence on 'Sabbath Observance' and point to the New Testament teaching that Christ 'fulfilled' the Mosaic law by his atoning death and victorious resurrection, and in the teaching he himself gave and commissioned his apostles to spell out. Christ himself in his incarnate life was "born under law to redeem those under law, that we might receive the full rights of sons" (Gal 4:4f), so it is the apostles who declare that the observance of 'special days' of any sort is not now legally incumbent on Christians, but left to individual conscience. At the same time the moral principles on which the Mosaic law rests are re-emphasised in the New Testament because they reflect the character of the Lawgiver himself.

For these reasons, Christians should think deeply about the benefit of a weekly 'special day', not only for themselves but for society as a whole. This is why it is their democratic duty, not indeed to attempt to impose their own distinctive views on others, but to persuade them about what is for the common good. Hence this booklet.

Norman Anderson

NOTE TO READERS

At various points in the booklet references to the "Report of the Committee of Inquiry into Proposals to Amend the Shops Act", Cmnd. 9376, are given. These are made, not by footnotes, but by an indication in the text of the relevant paragraph(s) in the Report.

1. SUMMARY

The Government has announced its intention to introduce legislation which removes all restrictions from trading hours, thereby permitting Sunday trading. Is Sunday trading an issue which matters? This booklet argues that it matters profoundly, not just for Christians but for society as a whole. It is not right for Christians to impose their views on others and this booklet does not suggest they should. However, it does argue that Christians, if they really love their neighbour, should do all they can to persuade others that it is important for society to set aside as special one day in the week - a day free for worship, rest and family. It examines first the biblical case of special interest to Christians. It then puts forward the economic, social, legal and ideological arguments against unrestricted Sunday trading. Six days are enough for commercial activity. One day should remain special, a day for the other priorities in life.

THE BIBLICAL CASE

Why keep Sunday special?

NOT because:

- Sunday is the New Testament Sabbath. In our view, it is not. The Sabbath was a sign of God's covenant and relationship with Old Testament Israel. The New Testament does not make Sunday a sign of God's new covenant relationship with his people in the same way as the Lord's Supper.
- It is a sin to work on Sunday. Working on Sunday is not necessarily sinful. Paul tells us that whether we keep Sunday special or not is a matter of individual conscience. Working on Sunday is only wrong if it leads us to neglect the underlying principles of love for God and love for our neighbour.
- There is a command by Jesus and the apostles to keep one day special. Both Jesus and the apostles did keep a day special in the week, but they nowhere make it a command to God's people.

So why keep Sunday special? Because:

- A day of rest is part of God's plan for all men. It is part of what is best for man. Setting Sunday apart helps ensure we make time in the week to rest.
- God cares deeply about family and community life. A day in the week when almost everybody is free from work is an important way to help family life and friendships to flourish, by giving people time to spend together.

1

- God cares for those with low incomes and little influence. A day in the week largely free from commercial activity is especially valuable to those who would otherwise run the risk of unfair treatment by employers.
- God requires that Christians show their love in regular meetings together, love for him in worship and for each other in fellowship. A weekly day set aside for this helps us greatly as Christians to honour God in this way.
- Where Sunday is different, this is a standing witness to the resurrection of Christ and his impact on the world. Where Christians treat Sunday as different, they make themselves distinctive in a pluralistic society, and proclaim that Christ is the risen Lord.
- For centuries now, Sunday has symbolized that, as a society, we aim to acknowledge God in our public life. If the church lets it go without a murmur, are we not saying to our society that whether God is acknowledged or ignored in our public life no longer concerns us?

While it may not be sin for a Christian to treat Sunday the same as every other day, it would be a sin if Christians were to stand silently by and allow many people to suffer, family life to deteriorate, and society to choose to ignore Christ. If we are not seeking to preserve these values by ensuring that Sunday remains a special day, how do we propose to do it?

THE ECONOMIC EFFECTS

The economic effects are not central to the Sunday trading debate. There will be economic effects but, whether they are positive or negative, they will be small. There are reasons, however, for believing they will be negative:

1. Estimates of the likely extent of Sunday opening vary. Although the number of shops which open may be small at first, it will almost certainly rise over time. Wherever a recession reduces turnover or a shop finds its market share is shrinking it will be under pressure to extend opening hours. If the premium paid for work on Sunday falls, which will happen if it is left to market forces, then Sunday opening will become more attractive. In many places Sunday may well become the second busiest shopping day of the week.

2. Total sales in the retail sector will rise very little, if at all, but costs will rise as shops will have to be staffed, heated and lighted for seven days instead of six. This will lead either to higher prices or lower profit margins, or something of both.

3. The effect on employment in retailing will depend on the change in total sales. The Institute for Fiscal Studies predicted that if sales do not rise, the equivalent of 20,000 jobs will be lost in the long run, but if sales rise by 2% there will be a gain of 9,000 jobs. However, these job increases will be offset either by a reduction in the funds available for investment or by job losses elsewhere.

4.   At present, the retail sector is highly competitive, but Sunday trading will drive many independent retailers out of business. As the dominance of multiple chain stores grows, these competitive conditions may in part be lost, to the detriment of both manufacturers and consumers.

5.   Some retailers, the DIY stores and some shops in tourist areas, will gain but the majority will probably lose. The market operates in such a way that many retailers will open even though collectively it would have been more profitable for them to stay shut. Consumers will gain from longer shopping hours, but lose out as their choice of establishment diminishes. It is difficult to argue that the benefits outweigh the costs

THE SOCIAL IMPLICATIONS

The church is often seen to be defending a narrow sectional interest whenever it protests against Sunday trading. However, Christian concern about Sunday trading extends well beyond its impact on church life. In time it will have deep and widespread effects on society as a whole.

1.   Family life will be damaged. People will be taken out of their homes on the one day when the rest of the family is most likely to be there. This will affect shopworkers first, but then other workers in services such as public transport, police, and waste disposal which will all be needed to support Sunday shopping. A million married women are shopworkers and there will be many who have to choose between keeping their jobs and being with their families.

2.   Shopworkers will suffer. Many shopworkers might object to Sunday work for family or religious reasons. However, with the possible exception of existing shopworkers, the Government does not intend to ensure Sunday work is voluntary. If told to work on Sundays by an employer, a shopworker will have to agree, or lose his job. Under seven day trading, shopworkers will need more protection, not less. However, their main form of protection, the Wages Council, may be abolished. The Auld Report states that if this happens, "there would be a strong likelihood of exploitation in the form of lower wages . . . and possibly in a longer working week". Keeping shops closed one day a week as the Shops Act did, while not primarily aimed at protecting shopworkers, has been one of the best ways of affording such protection.

3.   Pensioners, and others on low incomes, will suffer hardship as local shops go out of business and longer journeys are needed to get to shops. Community life will decay as villages lose these shops.

4.   Residents near shopping centres will lose their one day of peace and quiet. Many will be deeply upset by this change in their lives.

5.   Alcohol is a major contributory factor in violent crimes and fatal road accidents. If we wish to restrict the times at which alcohol may be purchased,

then we will need to keep restrictions on trading hours.

6.   The character of our democracy will be undermined. An issue which has always been regarded as a question of conscience to be decided on a free vote will have been made party policy. A major social change will have been introduced by the Government even though it never mentioned such an intention in its manifesto. These are precedents which point away from government accountability and towards greater state control. On top of this Parliament will be making a symbolic statement that it no longer wants Christian values to influence its legislation. What values will we put in their place?

7.   Many people argue that Scotland's experience, where Sunday trading is allowed, shows that the disruption and social damage it causes is small. However, as the Auld Committee themselves state, for a variety of clear reasons, Scotland is an unreliable guide to what is likely to happen in England. The same is true of Sweden and Massachusetts.

8.   Church life will be weakened. It will be harder for the church family to meet as a whole. Parking will often be difficult in towns and cities, and church services will be disturbed by noise. The first steps of faith will be harder to take because there will be so many distractions to keep people from ever coming to church. As the Christian community is marginalised, further moral decay in society may follow.

9.   Sunday is at present a day which people value as different. It will steadily become like all the rest. Sunday serves as a marker in the rhythm of life, a rhythm which will give way to monotony for many people. Once Sunday is lost it will be very hard to recover.

THE LEGAL ARGUMENTS

The case for the abolition of restrictions on trading hours is often made on legal grounds. The legal arguments may be answered as follows:

1.   The existing law is full of anomalies and ambiguities. BUT the anomalies are trivial compared with the social issues at stake. They are of little operational significance and are generally cited just to score points in the debate. In any case, with imagination and thoroughness, they can largely be put right. The ambiguities, where they exist, have arisen because the Shops Act 1950 is poorly drafted. They argue for a new Act which is more carefully drawn up, not the abolition of all restrictions as proposed by the Government.

2.   The law is openly defied by shopkeepers. There are blatant infringements of the law, BUT these are perpetrated by a narrow section of the retail trade, notably the DIY and garden centres. Some 93 per cent of shopkeepers in surveys in 42 towns across England and Wales were found to be closed. Only 1.4 per cent of the shops surveyed were open illegally. Infringements might

constitute a case for limited and selective relaxation of the law, but not for total abolition.

3.   Enforcement by local authorities is uneven and unfair. BUT local authorities are hamstrung in their enforcement duty because the maximum penalty for infringement of the law is so small that it has no deterrent impact. The answer is to increase penalties to realistic levels, not to dismantle the law entirely.

4.   The law must go because it is unacceptable to the majority of people. This is an unproved assertion. The opinion polls on which this conclusion is reached can be shown to be unreliable and inconsistent and unable to demonstrate substantial proven demand for widespread Sunday trading.

5.   It is inappropriate to use the criminal law to restrict trading hours. BUT this is not true. Provided the law is well-drafted, and proves enforceable, it is more appropriate to use the criminal law than the civil law. The criminal law concerns itself with offences against society, including motoring and trading offences, and the civil law with wrongs against individuals. Widespread shop opening will harm large groups in society and our way of life as a whole, not just certain individuals.

6.   There is no viable alternative to abolition of restrictions. This has been the trump card of those in favour of abolition so far BUT this conclusion rests on an analysis of the alternatives which is superficial and one-sided in many places. A number of alternatives have been suggested, and if they were carefully refined and developed, they would prove enforceable and acceptable. There are at least ten countries in Europe which find themselves capable of enforcing a general prohibition on Sunday trading. The issue is not one of legal feasibility but of political will.

THE IDEOLOGICAL ISSUES

The case for the abolition of restrictions on trading hours is often made on ideological grounds. Restrictions must go if we are to develop a free economy. Consumers and traders should be free to buy and sell what they want, when they want. These arguments are less persuasive when examined:

1.   The free economy argument. BUT even on purely economic grounds, a free economy does not necessarily function perfectly, and in this instance economic theory suggests Sunday trading is unlikely to enhance economic welfare. A free economy has no built-in mechanism to ensure that a just outcome is generated. Moreover, the free economy relies on certain moral values for its efficient functioning, but is unable by itself to nurture these moral values.

2.   The freedom of choice argument. BUT if trading hours are not restricted then the freedom to make one's family or faith a priority will be restricted. Sunday trading pampers to the material *wants* of consumers and traders but

5

at the expense of the human *needs* of shopworkers and others. Freedom of choice is good for man, but it is better for him to love God, and to love his neighbour.

CONCLUSION

There is a strong case against unrestricted Sunday trading. Moreover, the issue has much wider implications than appear at first sight. It serves as a signpost for the direction in which our society is moving: open disregard for the church, increasing pressure on family life, indifference to deteriorating conditions of work, lack of government accountability, increased power for the big business at the expense of the small independent, and a higher premium on a market philosophy than on people and their human needs.

Christians should not impose their views on others, but they should do all they can to persuade others of the benefits of Christian morality out of concern for the welfare of others and a refusal to allow God's truth to go unheard. There is still time to persuade people of all the positive benefits of keeping Sunday special. Christians and all those with Christian sympathies can make a difference. If they want to.

2. INTRODUCTION

There has been some form of legal restriction on commercial activity on Sunday ever since the Fairs and Markets Act of 1448, and possibly before.[1] The special nature of Sunday, one of Britain's oldest traditions, is currently maintained by the Shops Act 1950. Along with subsequent case law and one or two minor Acts, this governs trading hours in England, Wales and Scotland. The Act rules that in England and Wales "Every shop shall . . . be closed for the serving of customers on Sunday". However, its Schedule Five contains a list of goods which are exempt from this general prohibition, including, for instance, newspapers, confectionery, fresh fruit and vegetables, milk and vehicle accessories. There are further exemptions in holiday resorts, and for Jewish shopkeepers who close on Saturdays. Such is the general character of the present law.

There have been nineteen attempts in all to reform and relax this law, thirteen in the last eight years. On every occasion so far, the proposals have been rejected by Parliament. Nonetheless, there is virtually no-one who considers the existing law entirely satisfactory. At the same time, there is deep and widespread disagreement on the nature and extent of the reform necessary.

There is a wide range of groups who want to see restrictions on Sunday trading retained. Among them are the churches, the shopworkers' union, USDAW, and many retailers, including high street names such as the John Lewis Partnership and Marks & Spencer, and the majority of small independent shops. A survey by the Association of Independent Retailers found that 83 per cent of small traders were opposed to the removal of all restrictions, and 62 per cent believed that the present restrictions on Sunday trading should stay.

Part of the retail trade, however, wants to see an end to restrictions. The greatest pressure is coming from the out-of-town DIY superstores, and, after this, stores such as W. H. Smith and Woolworths which have DIY subsidiaries, but also from other stores such as Debenhams. In addition, certain Government departments, namely the Home Office, the Treasury and the Department of Trade and Industry, currently favour liberalisation.

Consumer opinion also appears to have shifted over the last few years in favour of Sunday trading. In the 1978 NOP Survey, 41 per cent of respondents were in favour of changes to allow shops to open for longer hours (weekdays and Sundays). A 1983 MORI poll produced a corresponding figure of 73 per cent. The National Consumer Council is pressing hard for deregulation. These results, however, conceal at least as much as they reveal. Another

---

[1] A memorandum from Latimer House, "Sunday Trade - A Christian Perspective" makes reference to an act regulating Sunday trading dating back to the reign of King Athelstan (925-941).

survey by the National Consumer Council in 1981 found that only one in ten respondents considered existing shopping hours inconvenient.

The Home Office in August 1983 set up a Committee of Inquiry, chaired by Mr. Robin Auld, QC, to examine proposals to amend the Shops Acts. Its terms of reference were:

"To consider what changes are needed in the Shops Acts, having regard to the interests of consumers, employers and employees and to the traditional character of Sunday and to make recommendations as to how these should be achieved."

The Committee approached its task by considering two questions. First, is there any justifiable purpose for restricting trading hours, any interest which deserves protection? Second, even if there is, can legislation be devised which could achieve that end? It based its answers on submissions of evidence by the whole spectrum of interest groups - consumers, unions, retailers, the churches, and so on. An independent economic review by the Institute for Fiscal Studies was also presented to the Committee.

The questions are considered at some length and the evidence is well-documented. Despite much evidence which points in the opposite direction, their Report concludes: "We are convinced that the removal of restrictions on trading hours offers the best - indeed the only - way forward" (para 289). The Report's major recommendation was therefore very simple: "the abolition in England, Wales and Scotland of all legal restrictions on the hours for which shops may be open to serve customers" (para 291). The Committee was of the view that any adverse effects such a move would cause would be "far outweighed by the substantial benefits that deregulation would bring" (para 289).

Events have now gone one step further. The House of Commons resolved, in a vote where Conservative MPs were under a three-line Whip: "That this House takes note of the Report . . . ; accepts the case for the removal of legislative limitations on shop hours; and looks forward to the Government bringing forward legislation to remove such limitations".[2] It surprised many that the Conservative Party did not allow a free vote (i.e. a vote of conscience) but required MPs to vote as instructed by the Party. It now seems certain that the Government will bring forward such legislation in the autumn of 1985 and, with their huge majority, these proposals could well become law by September 1986. This will only be prevented if the Government, or many individual MPs, can be persuaded that there is substantial opposition to the proposed changes from a significant proportion of the electorate.

The Government's proposals are not the result of widespread clamour for the abolition of restrictions. The pressure for abolition springs from three main sources. First, there is a desire to be rid of a law which has proved an irritation to many because of its shortcomings, and abolition is regarded as a simpler solution than sensible reform. Second, there is the prevailing political

---

[2] House of Commons, Official Report, 20 May 1985, Vol. 79, No. 120, col. 745

philosophy which generates a strong desire to give full rein to the free market. Third, there is the persistent lobbying of a number of highly motivated interest groups, above all DIY centres and out-of-town stores, which stand to gain millions of pounds in turnover. If these get their way, it will be at the expense of much of what we value in British society, and will involve increased burdens for many. Sunday will no longer be a 'different day', freedom to worship will be impaired and family life will be harmed. Shopworkers, small shopkeepers, pensioners and others on low incomes will all suffer.

Despite all this, Christians have been slow and unsure in their response. This is partly because the theological position of Sunday is itself a matter of debate among Christians. The nineteenth century view was that Sunday has replaced the Old Testament Sabbath as part of the Ten Commandments. At the other extreme are those who believe Sabbaths or Sundays no longer have any relevance for the Christian who has been set free from the Law. However, we believe that the majority of Christians through the centuries have held a position which lies somewhere between these poles. The first section examines the theological issues raised by the Sunday trading debate and presents a biblical case for society keeping Sunday special.

Even among Christians who are convinced on theological grounds of the value of Sunday as a special day, many have not been able to enter the public debate effectively. Involvement is hampered by ignorance. The social and economic implications are not immediately apparent. The Auld Committee concluded that the benefits of Sunday trading would far outweigh the costs. However, as the British Council of Churches saw, there is "a serious conflict between the evidence they present and the conclusion they reach".[3] The facts of the matter show that the costs will far outweigh the benefits but so far the arguments which demonstrate it is neither advisable nor necessary to abolish restrictions have not been readily accessible. The following four sections examine the economic, social, legal and ideological aspects of the Sunday trading debate. They aim to help Christians think through every dimension of the issue so that they can discuss it in a way which is relevant and convincing to those who do not profess a Christian faith.

The last stumbling block is a reluctance to try to influence policies. Some feel it is 'worldly' to get involved in politics. Others believe that to take a stand on Sunday trading is an improper attempt to 'impose' Christian views on others. The constant theme of this booklet, however, is that it is to society's benefit to set aside Sunday as a special day. As conscientious citizens, Christians have a responsibility and a right to express their view. But there is more to it than this. If 56 million people are about to take a turning which will be to their detriment, involvement to prevent this is not 'worldliness' but love for one's neighbour.

We should not 'impose' Christian values on others. It would not work in any case. However, if there are good reasons for making Sunday a special day,

[3] British Council of Churches and Free Church Federal Council, "A Critique of the Auld Report", para 1. (Available on request from B.C.C. or F.C.F.C.).

and if God's word tells us this too, then we should do all we can to *persuade* men of this fact. It is the same with trying to persuade men to believe in Christ - there are good reasons for such belief and God's word tells us what they are. It is not a question of 'imposing' views on others, but one of contending for the truth. Our hope is that this booklet will generate careful thought and concerted action by all those who are concerned to promote family life, protect the weak, and maintain the nation's Christian heritage.

3. SABBATH AND SUNDAY IN THE BIBLE

GENESIS 2:2-3

"By the seventh day God had finished the work he had been doing; so on the seventh day he rested from all his work. And God blessed the seventh day and made it holy, because on it he rested from all the work of creating that he had done."

Teaching about rest in the Bible begins at creation. It occurs immediately after the account in Genesis chapter one about the making of man. This is before the Fall, and long before Israel is chosen by God from among the nations. The principle of creative activity followed by rest is rooted in the person of God and is not simply a concession to the frailty of man.

There is no explicit command here to observe a Sabbath rest. Like the institution of marriage, the day of rest is not commanded for man. A creation ordinance is not an order. Rather it is an institution for the welfare and good of man which God has built into the way things are. It is the way the human mechanism works best.

It seems God was resting from the seventh day onwards. His creative activity was not an endless cycle of work followed by rest. Adam and Eve in the Garden of Eden were living in the seventh day of rest which, before the Fall, stretched eternally forwards. When man sinned, man ceased to be in that state of rest. So God said that from that moment his life would be characterized by toil (Gen 3:17-19). After the Fall, the Sabbath day of rest was a day of remembering the rest forfeited in the Fall.

God not only blessed the seventh day, he also made it holy. Holy means special, different or set apart. Part of God's purpose was to make one day special "because on that day he rested from his work of creating that he had done". If God chose to rest, and blessed the day of rest, we are losing one of God's great blessings to man if we do not follow God's prescribed rhythm of life. Following the French and Russian revolutions, various alternatives to the pattern of six days of work followed by one of rest were tested. On each occasion they failed. A seven day rhythm in life is what God designed for man. We ignore it at our own cost.

11

EXODUS 20:8-11

"Remember the Sabbath day by keeping it holy. Six days you shall labour and do all your work, but the seventh day is a Sabbath to the LORD your God. On it you shall not do any work, neither you, nor your son or daughter, nor your manservant or maidservant, nor your animals, nor the alien within your gates. For in six days the LORD made the heavens and the earth, the sea, and all that is in them, but he rested on the seventh day. Therefore the LORD blessed the Sabbath day and made it holy."

This and the next two passages are taken from the Law. In total there are at least twelve different passages in the Law which deal with the Sabbath explicitly. In addition, there are many other passages which contain the 'rest' principle, such as those which require that in every seventh year the land is given rest (Lev 25:1-7). All this points to the importance attached to the Sabbath rest concept in biblical revelation. As well as noting what the law teaches in this way, we also have to search behind it to discover what God's purpose was when he gave the law.

This is the Fourth Commandment, so it has a special place in Old Testament revelation. Only the Ten Commandments were written by 'the finger of God' on to the Tablets of Stone from the blazing mountain, and only they were revealed directly to the whole asembly of the people. God clearly attached great importance to this particular part of the Old Testament law.

The reason given to the Israelites in this law is traced back to creation (Gen 2:2-3). God made the Sabbath a day for Israel to remember that God had rested from his work in creation. It had been special in his work of creation, and it was to be special to Israel. Six days are allowed for work. That is enough. If an Israelite was so busy he could not manage all his work in six days, he was too busy. The Sabbath law was a guard against materialism - against becoming so absorbed in work that there was no time to relax or think about God. It challenges us too - are we too busy to give the best of our time to God?

The law is addressed to the family elder. He is responsible to make sure the whole of his family and household carry it out. It is a *household* law, not just a matter of individual conscience. The household includes servants and even animals. The Sabbath was a family event, and still is among Jews who celebrate it with a family meal. It was a part of the whole system of Old Testament law which aimed to prevent the extended family group from disintegrating in the course of economic growth. The Jubilee laws on land (Lev 25:10), the Year of Debt Remission (Deut 15:1-6) and the ban on interest

(Deut 23:19-20) all would have kept land and capital within the extended family framework.

If a principle of the Sabbath law was to keep time aside for worship and the family, then Christians are applying the principle in society today when they seek to preserve the law against Sunday trading. For if Sunday trading is introduced, the families of many of the two million workers and more involved in retailing and supporting services in Britain will not have even one day of the week when they are all at home together. For many families, the tradition of 'Sunday dinner', and of gardening or other activities around the home together, will be destroyed as one or other member of the family will be out working. Will we then be surprised if divorce rates continue to escalate, and neglected children bring violence to the streets?

"Then the LORD said to Moses:
'Say to the Israelites, "You must observe my Sabbaths. This will be a sign
between me and you for the generations to come, so that you may know that I am
the LORD, who makes you holy.
' "Observe the Sabbath, because it is holy to you. Anyone who desecrates it
must be put to death; whoever does any work on that day must be cut off from his
people. For six days work is to be done, but the seventh day is a Sabbath of rest,
holy to the LORD. Whoever does any work on the Sabbath day must be put to
death. The Israelites are to observe the Sabbath, celebrating it for the
generations to come as a lasting covenant. It will be a sign between me and the
Israelites for ever, for in six days the LORD made the heavens and the earth, and
on the seventh day he abstained from work and rested." '
When the LORD finished speaking to Moses on Mount Sinai, he gave him the
two tablets of the Testimony, the tablets of stone inscribed by the finger of God."

This passage is strategically placed. It comes right at the end of the forty days and nights which Moses spent on Mount Sinai with God receiving the Law. It is God's 'last word' on how he wants his relationship with the Israelites to be ordered.

The primary significance of the Sabbath for an Israelite was as a *sign of that relationship - the covenant*. The Sabbath is not just about the Lord's mastery over our use of time, or man's need to rest. It has an overriding importance in the Old Testament as a signpost or reminder of the special covenant relationship between God and the nation of Israel (see Ezek 20:11-12). It is this role of the Sabbath which so obviously has to change in the New Testament. The new covenant had new signs and symbols - the bread and the wine, baptism and, in a sense, the Cross.

The fact that the Sabbath is a sign of the covenant as a whole explains why the death penalty was required for those who broke it. The death penalty today seems so severe, especially when it applied to somebody who just went out to collect wood for a fire (Num 15:32ff). However, the Sabbath for an Israelite was not an optional extra. To break it was to insult God publicly, to reject him as King, to repudiate his rule over society. As the Sabbath was a sign of the covenant, like circumcision, to break the rules was equivalent to a rejection of Israel's special relationship with God.

DEUTERONOMY 5:12-15

"Observe the Sabbath day by keeping it holy, as the LORD your God has commanded you. Six days you shall labour, and do all your work, but the seventh day is a Sabbath to the LORD your God. On it you shall not do any work, neither you, nor your son or daughter, nor your manservant or maidservant, nor your ox, your donkey or any of your animals, nor the alien within your gates, so that your manservant and maidservant may rest, as you do. Remember that you were slaves in Egypt and that the LORD your God brought you out of there with a mighty hand and an outstretched arm. Therefore, the LORD your God has commanded you to observe the Sabbath day."

The Ten Commandments are stated twice in the Old Testament law. The second time is in the passage above, in Deuteronomy. There are just a small number of important differences in the two accounts, and the main one is in the Sabbath commandment. In Exodus, the reason given for 'remembering the Sabbath' is that of God's work in creation: in Deuteronomy the link is with Israel's redemption from slavery in the land of Egypt.

The emphasis on release from slavery in Egypt helps to explain the requirement that the whole household, including servants, should not work on the Sabbath. The Israelites knew what it was like to be forced to work seven days a week to earn a living, and to have no defence from the threats of employers. The Sabbath was a kind of 'Employee Protection Act' in Israel. It was a constitutional means of protecting workers from being exploited through overwork.

What is the relevance of this in Britain today? If the law limiting Sunday trading in Britain is a source of protection for employees, Christians are obeying one of the principles behind the Deuteronomic law in trying to preserve this law in Britain today. The Auld Committee, which in 1984 recommended to the Government that the Sunday trading law should be abolished, considered that "a statutory provision specifically protecting shopworkers from being required to work against their will on Sundays and late at night would be impracticable ..." If Sunday trading is permitted, many workers are likely to feel pressure to work on Sundays to keep their jobs, although for many this is the only day of the week when the family can be together. Those on low incomes are likely to feel this pressure most acutely. There is no source of protection for them against this pressure to work unsocial hours. The choice between family and job will affect around one million married women who work in retailing, if they are asked to work on Sunday. If Sunday trading is allowed, step by step, people in every industry might be forced to work, making it increasingly difficult for husbands and wives to be sure of having one day a week together. This must surely be of concern to Christians.

AMOS 8:4-8

"Hear this, you who trample the needy and do away with the poor of the land, saying, 'When will the New Moon be over that we may sell grain, and the Sabbath be ended that we may market wheat?' skimping the measure, boosting the price, and cheating with dishonest scales, buying the poor with silver and the needy for a pair of sandals, selling even the sweepings with the wheat. The LORD has sworn by the Pride of Jacob: 'I will never forget anything they have done. Will not the land tremble for this, and all who live in it mourn?' "

Through Amos, God declares the imminence of divine judgement, first against neighbouring heathen nations for their crimes towards humanity (Amos 1:3 - 2:3), then against Judah (Amos 2:4-5), and finally against Israel (Amos 2: 6-16), for their disobedience to God's revelation.

This passage is the fourth of five visions of the judgement God plans to bring on to his people Israel. Earlier in this passage, Israel is pictured as a basket of ripe fruit, ripe for judgement because the people oppress the poor.

Why are the retailers in Israel so keen for the Sabbath to be over, and why is it wrong? Amos pictures these businessmen as being concerned about one thing, and one thing only - money. They have no interest in honouring God by observing the Sabbath; rather they want to see it over as rapidly as possible so they can get on with their business. They have little concern for honesty and integrity in their business dealings, and none at all for the poor in society who are harmed by their activities.

Although the large retailers today pressing for Sunday trading are not necessarily "boosting the price" or "cheating with dishonest scales", surely they are guilty on two other counts implicit in this passage. Firstly, they have no regard for the importance of Sunday as a day of worship, and therefore show little interest for God's claims on their lives. There is talk that they may even offer special discounts for Sunday shopping to draw people into the shops and out of their homes and perhaps away from the churches. Such is their pursuit of the profit motive.

Secondly, they are showing no concern for 'the poor', the lower income groups who will be hurt by Sunday trading. This includes low income shopworkers, and those working in other supporting services, who will have to work on Sundays whether they like it or not, because they cannot afford to lose their jobs. It includes tens of thousands of small retailers who will have to work seven days a week to maintain sales levels, many of whom will be driven out of business by this extra pressure according to the Auld Committee. As these shops disappear, many of the disabled and pensioners will no longer be able to shop locally but will have to travel further to an impersonal supermarket to do their shopping. This will impose expense and hardship on those least able to bear it.

The word of judgement is ominous. The picture of fruit ripe for judgement speaks of the culmination of a long process. In Britain we have seen a steady erosion of Christian morality, as sexual licence has grown more acceptable, divorce more common, and abortion more freely available. Now we want to add a more visible rejection of 'traditional' Christian morality by doing away with Sunday. The judgement predicted by Amos did not fall only on those actively responsible. It fell on all who lived in the land.

"If you keep your feet from breaking the Sabbath
And from doing as you please on my holy day,
If you call the Sabbath a delight
And the LORD'S holy day honourable,
And if you honour it by not going your own way
And not doing as you please or speaking idle words,
Then you will find your joy in the LORD,
And I will cause you to ride on the heights of the land
And to feast on the inheritance of your father Jacob.
The mouth of the LORD has spoken."

Amos, Isaiah, Jeremiah, Ezekiel, all have much to say about the Sabbath. As prophets, their mandate was to call people back to the Law which God has given through Moses to the Jewish people. Over and over again, they upbraid the Israelites for making the Sabbath a normal business day, and specifically for carrying out trading activities. It is one of the major social themes taken up by these prophets. However, it is addressed both to illustrate the way in which the quality of Israel's relationship with God was impaired, and as an issue of social justice.

Calvin believed that keeping the Sabbath in the Old Testament involved self-denial. This passage seems to support his view. The first line puts the emphasis on our actions. It is not enough to say that we honour God. Whether we do or not is shown by the way in which we live. As the rest of the chapter shows, Isaiah is not thinking of fasting or asceticism when he speaks of self-denial, but of "feeding the hungry and satisfying the needs of the oppressed" (Is 58:10-11). The Lord's Day is meant to be specially dedicated to acts of mercy.

What do these promises refer to? There are three promises here if "we call the Lord's holy day honourable":
1. *You will find your joy in the Lord.* If we set aside time properly to take delight in the Lord, he will become the chief source of our joy.
2. *I will cause you to ride on the heights of the land.* 'Ride' refers to Israel as a military conqueror, recapturing the fortresses and cities such as Jerusalem positioned on the mountains and hills, which were probably in Babylonian hands at the time Isaiah wrote.
3. *And to feast on the inheritance of your father Jacob.* If they recapture the land, they will be able to feast on the abundant food available in their own land.

How can we apply these promises to ourselves? If we as individuals honour God in our way of life and our worship, then we will find the Lord is our chief source of joy. No doubt this is true, but the primary fulfilment of their promises is not in the life of an individual, but in the life of a community. Isaiah was not addressing individuals when he wrote, but a whole people. If a society patterns its life on the word of God today, by keeping one day special for his worship, surely God will remember his promises given originally to Israel, 'by which man shall live'.

Christians today are often reluctant to speak of God's concern for Britain as a country. Memories of German nationalism and where it led are still fresh in our minds. But the Bible often speaks of God's concern for the nations. He sets their boundaries and their times (Acts 17:26). As Jesus died for people of all nations (Jn 3:16), it is reasonable to believe that he loves all the nations equally, although perhaps Israel still occupies a special place in God's providence (Rom 11:28-29). Nations make certain decisions collectively in their national assembly or Parliament, and God holds them accountable collectively for those decisions (Prov 14:34; Ps 94:10).

So even today, God is concerned with Britain as a nation, and with the laws which our national representatives in Parliament make to govern us. For centuries, our law has been built upon Christian traditions. If we remove that foundation, what will we put in its place?

"In those days I saw men in Judah treading winepresses on the Sabbath and bringing in grain and loading it on donkeys, together with wine, grapes, figs and all other kinds of loads. And they were bringing all this into Jerusalem on the Sabbath. Therefore I warned them against selling food on that day. Men from Tyre who lived in Jerusalem were bringing in fish and all kinds of merchandise and selling them in Jerusalem on the Sabbath to the people of Judah. I rebuked the nobles of Judah and said to them, 'What is this wicked thing you are doing - desecrating the Sabbath day? Didn't your forefathers do the same things, so that our God brought all this calamity upon us and upon this city? Now you are stirring up more wrath against Israel by desecrating the Sabbath.'

When evening shadows fell on the gates of Jerusalem before the Sabbath, I ordered the doors to be shut and not opened until the Sabbath was over. I stationed some of my own men at the gates so that no load could be brought in on the Sabbath day. Once or twice the merchants and sellers of all kinds of goods spent the night outside Jerusalem. But I warned them and said, 'Why do you spend the night by the wall? If you do this again, I will lay hands on you.' From that time on they no longer came on the Sabbath. Then I commanded the Levites to purify themselves and go and guard the gates in order to keep the Sabbath day holy."

What happened? This incident occurred late in Old Testament history, in about 450 BC, after the Israelites had returned from captivity in Babylon. The Sabbath law was being widely disregarded in the agricultural processing industry and retail distribution. The men of Judah were involved; so also were men of Tyre resident in Jerusalem, who were bringing goods from outside Jerusalem and selling them in the city, thus leading the locals astray. Nehemiah did not just enforce the law. He took action to prevent the possibility of its being broken. When certain traders took to camping outside the wall of the city during the Sabbath, either to gain public sympathy for their cause or to find a way to do their trade despite the ban, Nehemiah moved them on.

Why was the Sabbath so important to Nehemiah? When the Jews went into exile, they lost much of their cultural distinctiveness. They could no longer go to the Temple or carry out the sacrifices, for example. They no longer even had a king. In this situation, the Sabbath came to have much greater importance as a mark of what was distinctively Jewish. The same was true for the Pharisees living under Roman occupation, although by then its observance had been taken to extremes.

What right did Nehemiah have to enforce the Sabbath? Nehemiah was a Jew. The Mosaic law still represented Israel's constitution. The Sabbath still represented this sign of the covenant. Thus, he was doing no more than enforce the law of the land, although many were out of sympathy with it. He could have turned a blind eye to it. But clearly he believed his attempt to lead people in the right direction would be pleasing to God (end of v 22).

Nehemiah's mandate came from the state as well as from God. Nehemiah had been given the position of leader of the remnant of Israel by God. His position had been endorsed by the Persian Empire, although it had been repeatedly challenged by Sanballat and others. Nehemiah was not living in a pluralistic society, governed by democratic decision-making processes. From God's point of view, Israel was still a theocracy, under a constitution given directly by God. From a human perspective, Nehemiah had been given a mandate to rule Israel according to the laws of his country, and had received popular acclaim from time to time for his work (e.g. Neh 5:13).

What right do Christians have to influence political decisions? In seeking the contemporary relevance of this passage for the Sabbath/Sunday discussion, we wish to focus on a single issue. On what basis can Christians seek to influence the social order? Marxists believe their actions are justified by the inevitable flow of history. Clearly, the Christian today has a mandate profoundly different from Nehemiah's. So what mandate do Christians have to attempt to steer the ship of state?

In the New Testament, the rule of Christ is seen to extend over all men. Whether men acknowledge it or not, Jesus is their Lord. This is not to say that all men *belong* to his kingdom, for unless a man is born again he cannot see the kingdom of God (Jn 3:3). But Christ asserts his rule over all men. He commands all men everywhere to repent (Acts 17:30). As creator of the world, as well as its redeemer, Christ has been given all authority in heaven and on earth (Matt 28:18). It is from Jesus as rightful ruler of the whole earth that Christians receive their mandate to influence political decisions, as it is Jesus who calls them to be salt and light in society (Matt 5:13-16). Indeed, Jesus warns that if salt loses its saltiness, "it is no longer good for anything, except to be thrown out and trampled by men" (Matt 5: 13).

Should Christians impose their views on non-Christians? If Christians have the authority of Christ to influence political decisions, does this mean they can force their views on other people. In church history, many have thought so, but we believe Jesus rejected the use of force to extend his kingdom when he had the opportunity to use it (e.g. Jn 18:36). However, being unable to 'impose our views' does not rule out all forms of political action. Christians can exercise their democratic right to vote and make their views known. They can also seek to persuade people that what they are saying is right. They can campaign and work to change public opinion in competition with all the other interest groups who are pressing their case.

After speaking about being salt and light, Jesus urges his disciples to "teach and obey the law" of God, for that will make them great in the kingdom (Matt 5:13-19). 'Teaching' in today's world means not just talking to friends and neighbours about the issue, but influencing people through the media and through MPs. It is by persuasion, as well as following ourselves the values and guidelines of God's word, that we will influence public opinion and the laws of our society. If we believe God's word is really what is best for man, love for our neighbour will make us want to fulfil our responsibility to make our national laws conform to his will.

MATTHEW 12:1-8

"At that time Jesus went through the cornfields on the Sabbath. His disciples were hungry and began to pick some ears of corn and eat them. When the Pharisees saw this, they said to him 'Look! Your disciples are doing what is unlawful on the Sabbath.' He answered, 'Haven't you read what David did when he and his companions were hungry? He entered the house of God, and he and his companions ate the consecrated bread - which was not lawful for them to do, but only for the priests. Or haven't you read in the Law that on the Sabbath the priests in the temple desecrate the day and yet are innocent? I tell you that one greater than the temple is here. If you had known what these words mean, 'I desire mercy, not sacrifice,' you would not have condemned the innocent. For the Son of Man is Lord of the Sabbath'."

So we come to the New Testament. With the coming of Jesus, the King, a new age dawned. The old covenant was not abolished, it was fulfilled. Jesus inaugurated a new relationship with man, which focussed not on the Jewish people but on those from any nation or race who acknowledge Jesus as Lord of their lives. This was to affect every area of life, including the Sabbath, as we shall see in the pages which follow.

In this passage, Jesus is criticized when his disciples pick the ears of corn, rub them between their hands and eat them. this may have been to pass the time or they may have been genuinely hungry. There is nothing in the Old Testament law which forbids this, unless this kind of gleaning is categorized as harvesting (in which case see Ex 34:21). However, it was contrary to a set of explanatory rules followed by the Pharisees called the *Halakah*. It was precisely these extra detailed rules to which Jesus was so opposed.

Jesus appeals to David's example. The special twelve loaves of fresh bread of the priests were laid out every Sabbath day on the table in the Tent of Meeting, in two rows of six each (Lev 24:5-8). It was these loaves which David ate when he and his men were being pursued by Saul and were extremely hungry (I Sam 21:1-6). Since the Old Testament scriptures did not condemn David, by implication neither should the Pharisees condemn Jesus' disciples. The important general principle seems to be that in cases of need, the ceremonial requirements of the Law can be set aside by God's people. Applying that principle today, concern to honour God by keeping Sunday special should not prevent shops selling prescriptions, petrol and basic food items which people are likely to need on an emergency basis.

Jesus also points out that priests work on the Sabbath (Lev 24:8-9; Num 28:9-10). Here, one Old Testament law appears to overrule another. This suggests some hierarchy of laws when an individual finds two competing laws governing his situation. The same choice was made when the Jews circumcised on the Sabbath (Jn 7:22-23). Those in a similar situation today would be clergymen, doctors and others involved in essential services, who have to work at the time of the church services.

Jesus then moves on to the attack. Why were the Pharisees condemning his disciples? Their criticism showed a lack of understanding of the fundamental principle of Old Testament interpretation, which is love. God is concerned that people show love for him and for each other, rather than simply following a set of rules. You cannot have love without rules, and you should not have rules without love.

"For the Son of Man is Lord of the Sabbath". So Jesus concludes the discussion. The Son of Man image is used particularly with reference to his future rule over the whole world, and his return in glory. Jesus is Lord even of the Sabbath. Here is the ultimate interpretive principle. If Jesus is Lord or ruler of the Sabbath, he can do as he likes with it. Preserve it, abolish it, transform it or turn it upside down. That is his prerogative. The key issue is what he did do. In his own ministry, he kept the Sabbath special, not in terms of following detailed rules but in giving regular priority to worship (Lk 4:16), and to acts of mercy (e.g. Mark 3:1-6). Jesus did not come to abolish the law, but to fulfil it (Matt 5:17). His own example helps us to understand what that means in practice with respect to the Sabbath. Other New Testament passages are also important in helping us know how to apply it today.

"Then he said to them, 'The Sabbath was made for man, not man for the Sabbath. So the Son of Man is Lord even of the Sabbath'. Another time he went into the synagogue, and a man with a shrivelled hand was there. Some of them were looking for a reason to accuse Jesus, so they watched him closely to see if he would heal him on the Sabbath. Jesus said to the man with the shrivelled hand, 'Stand up in front of everyone.' Then Jesus asked them, 'Which is lawful on the Sabbath: to do good or to do evil, to save life or to kill?' But they remained silent. He looked round at them in anger and, deeply distressed at their stubborn hearts, said to the man, 'Stretch out your hand.' He stretched it out, and his hand was completely restored. Then the Pharisees went out and began to plot with the Herodians how they might kill Jesus."

Mark's account of the life of Jesus also contains the incident of the disciples passing through the field and picking off the heads of the wheat to eat them. The account is slightly shorter than in Matthew, and is followed by the healing of the man with a shrivelled hand, as it is in Matthew's gospel. However, Mark records several important additional points which are not in Matthew's account.

Jesus' famous statement, "The Sabbath was made for man, not man for the Sabbath" was made during the grain-eating incident. For those who see no further role for any sort of special day of rest, this saying presents a problem. Jesus asserts that the Sabbath was made for man. He did not say, "The Sabbath was made for the Jews". It contains something important for all men. This passage seems to point back to the creation ordinance, which, as we have noted, was not a command but a fact about how life for man is best ordered. The principle of rest, and a rhythm of life based on a seven-day pattern, is part of what is best for man. There is no way round it. If we ignore it, we do it at cost to ourselves. If we love our neighbour, we will want to see it built into the structure of our own societies.

Jesus insists he is Lord of the Sabbath. The issue shifts here away from purely legal questions to the person of Jesus himself. The logic of the passage is not immediately clear. But Jesus seems to be saying, "The fact that I have the right to put man's needs over the ceremonial requirements of the law points to my Lordship over the ceremonial law". Jesus is not doing away with the Sabbath here. Nowhere does he abolish it or degrade it. He only wants to ensure it is interpreted and used in its proper place.

One more important principle governing Sabbath observance is stated here, which undoubtedly applies to the whole of the Law. "Which is lawful to do on the Sabbath: to do good or to do evil, to save life or to kill?" This points again to a hierarchy of laws. Love must govern our interpretation and application of any rule given to us in God's word. If the strictness of Sabbath observance led to a refusal to carry out acts of mercy, something was wrong with the interpretation. Surely there is something equally wrong with our interpetation today if our failure to keep one day in seven special leads to the opposite of acts of mercy, that is, to active discrimination against those who depend on their weekly day off for the opportunity to worship and to rest.

"On a Sabbath Jesus was teaching in one of the synagogues, and a woman was there who had been crippled by a spirit for eighteen years. She was bent over and could not straighten up at all. When Jesus saw her, he called her forward and said to her, 'Woman, you are set free from your infirmity'. Then he put his hands on her, and immediately she straightened up and praised God. Indignant because Jesus had healed on the Sabbath, the synogugue ruler said to the people, 'There are six days for work. So come and be healed on those days, not on the Sabbath'.

The Lord answered him, 'You hypocrites! Doesn't each of you on the Sabbath untie his ox or donkey from the stall and lead it out to give it water? Then should not this woman, a daughter of Abraham, whom Satan has kept bound for eighteen long years, be set free on the Sabbath day from what bound her?' When he said all this, all his opponents were humiliated, but the people were delighted with all the wonderful things he was doing."

In Luke's gospel, an incident relating to the Sabbath is recorded which is not found in any of the other gospels. A woman for eighteen years has suffered by being crippled. She was bent over and could not straighten up at all. With no concern for the individual, the synagogue ruler tells the people to "come back tomorrow" if they want healing, as healing could be done on any day of the week. In his understanding of the Sabbath, people should avoid coming for healing on the Sabbath in case it made God angry. So what kind of God did he believe in? Certainly not the God who told Isaiah that he wanted acts of mercy rather than sacrifice (Is 58:6-9).

Jesus is angry. He points out the ruler's double standards by appealing to commonly-accepted behaviour. The ruler does not use the Sabbath as an excuse to prevent the normal course of humane kindness to animals. Animals *could* be left unwatered for a day, but it was kinder to take them out every day. If the Pharisees will untie an animal to take it to water on a Sabbath, why should he not 'untie' a woman who has been in bondage to Satan for eighteen years? For this work of the kingdom, for acts of love and mercy, every day is exactly the same and equally appropriate.

JOHN 5:16-18

"So, because Jesus was doing these things on the Sabbath, the Jews persecuted him. Jesus said to them, 'My Father is always at his work to this very day, and I, too, am working.' For this reason the Jews tried all the harder to kill him; not only was he breaking the Sabbath, but he was even calling God his own Father, making himself equal with God."

As with so many themes in Jesus' ministry, John's treatment of the Sabbath issue differs in many ways from that of other writers. John notes that Jesus heals on the Sabbath, but the implications for his claims to be the Messiah are appreciated more fully by the relatively sophisticated audience in Jerusalem. As a result, the debate revolves more around Jesus' claims and his work.

On this occasion, Jesus has just healed a man on the Sabbath day. He found the man lying by the Pool of Bethesda, rather than the man coming and finding him. Jesus commanded the man to pick up his mat and walk. The Pharisees were angry because carrying the mat on the Sabbath was against their rules. When Jesus uses the opportunity presented by this controversy to stress his claims of divinity, the Pharisees become even more angry.

Jesus asserts that God has been, and still is, "working", even up to that very day. How does this fit in with God's rest at creation? Of course, God cannot have been totally inactive since creation! He sustains all things by the word of his power (Heb 1:3). So God rested from his work in making the world (creation), but up to that time had not rested from his spiritual work of salvation. John's definition of "work" in his gospel always carries the broader idea of all that Jesus is saying and doing to bring salvation to man.

At his death on the Cross, Jesus cries, "It is finished", so after that God is no longer at his salvation-work in the same way. At the moment of the Resurrection we have God's second great act of salvation; in this the Sabbath is fulfilled, and a period of eternal salvation-rest is inaugurated. In the Old Testament, the Sabbath is a commemoration of deliverance from Egypt; in the New Testament, Sundays commemorate our deliverance from Satan. So there is a transfer from the seventh day to the first day of the week as the special day for the Christian.

Does the salvation-rest of God mean that humanity's weekly physical day of rest is no longer relevant or important? There is no longer the legal requirement of the Old Testament law when the Sabbath was rigorously enforced as a sign of God's special relationship with his people. Until his death and Resurrection the incarnate Christ, as part of the people Israel, lived under the old covenant, and so it is the apostles, not he, who state explicitly that treating Sunday as special is a question of individual conscience. However, to keep Sunday special helps us to commemorate the Resurrection as the moment of our deliverance from Satan and the inauguration of our salvation-rest. It is not mandatory to remember it in this way, but it is helpful.

ACTS 20:7

"On the first day of the week we came together to break bread. Paul spoke to the people . . ."

1 CORINTHIANS 16:1-2

"Now about the collection for God's people. Do what I told the Galatian churches to do. On the first day of every week, each of you should set aside a sum of money in keeping with his income, saving it up, so that when I come no collections will have to be made."

From the gospels, we move on to the period of the early church. What would be the attitude of the new church leaders to the Sabbath? Jewish Christians seem to have kept the Sabbath themselves generally, from the limited evidence available. However, the Sabbath became a burning issue when it became necessary to decide whether Gentile Christians living in pagan societies should observe it. The following passages in Acts and the Epistles have to be understood against this broader background.

These are the only two references to the first day of the week as having been kept as in any way special in the New Testament. The narrative in Acts is about the church in Troas. Luke makes worship on the first day of the week sound like a regular event, but does not make this explicit. When the Corinthians reference is added, it makes it probable that the first day of the week was widely regarded as special in some way by Christians in the early church.

In Deuteronomy, the Sabbath law was linked with Israel's redemption from slavery in the land of Egypt. The Sabbath was a weekly celebration of their great deliverance. It is this theme which lies primarily behind Christians changing the day from the Sabbath to "the first day of the week". For it was on the first day that Jesus rose from the dead and delivered Christians from their slavery to sin and death. So there is an obvious New Testament parallel in keeping the first day of the week as a special day of celebration.

There is no evidence for a weekly service by Christians apart from the verse in Acts. At the very beginning of our church, the disciples went daily to the Temple to pray. Paul often attended Jewish Sabbath services in order to take them his message. In Hebrews, the church is enjoined "not to give up meeting together" (Heb 10:25). However, there is no passage in the New Testament which instructs Christians to observe a day of rest, to celebrate the first day of the week or to keep the Sabbath.

The Corinthian passage is not about collective worship, but refers to something done at home. The calculation of income, and setting aside a gift, is an act of mercy, much in keeping with Jesus' own miracles, as the money was going to poor church members in another area. It would be highly appropriate to do this on a day set aside in some special way to the Lord, just as Jesus himself carried out special acts of mercy on the Sabbath. It is possible that Paul says they are to do it on the first day of the week because this was the local pay-day, but it seems more likely that this was the day the churches had set aside in some special way for their service to God. Note also that the first day of the week was special not just to the Corinthian church, but to the Galatian churches as well.

Some have argued from these verses that the first day of the week was the New Testament equivalent of the Old Testament Sabbath. Just as the Passover is fulfilled in the Lord's Supper, and circumcision in baptism, so the Sabbath is fulfilled in Sundays. Although this is a neat and tidy solution, there is no explicit New Testament warrant for it. While the Lord's Supper is inaugurated with such solemnity, we search in vain for any inauguration of the Lord's Day in the New Testament, or any command to keep it. What we find is rather the opposite - strenuous efforts by Paul to ensure the Sabbaths and festivals are not treated in the same way as in the Old Testament (see notes on texts in Romans, Galatians and Colossians).

The theological differences between those who take Sunday to be the New Testament Sabbath equivalent and those who do not may not make so much difference in practice. Many in both groups will want to honour God in their use of time on one day in the week, avoid negative legalism and promote a positive approach to acts of love and mercy on one day of the week which is set aside in a special way to honour the Lord Jesus. They only choose Sunday because it is the day Christ rose from the dead, and because the apostles themselves appear to have kept the first day of the week as special in a number of ways.

"Accept him whose faith is weak, without passing judgement on disputable matters. One man's faith allows him to eat everything, but another man, whose faith is weak, eats only vegetables. The man who eats everything must not look down on him who does not, and the man who does not eat everything must not condemn the man who does, for God has accepted him. Who are you to judge someone else's servant? To his own master he stands or falls. And he will stand, for the Lord is able to make him stand.

One man considers one day more sacred than another; another man considers every day alike. Each one should be fully convinced in his own mind. He who regards one day as special, does so to the Lord. He who eats meat, eats to the Lord, for he gives thanks to God; and he who abstains, does so to the Lord and gives thanks to God. For none of us lives to himself alone and none of us dies to himself alone. If we live, we live to the Lord; and if we die, we die to the Lord. So, whether we live or die, we belong to the Lord."

Paul, in his letter to the Romans, has examined in depth the basis of man's salvation as lying in the atoning death of Christ. Man is accepted through faith and not by the works of the law. In the final part of the book, Paul tackles a number of thorny political and social issues. The two brought together in this passage are concerned with whether it is right for Christians to eat meat offered to idols, and whether Christians should observe special 'days'. Paul may be only referring to the monthly and annual Jewish festivals here. However, this seems unlikely in view of the reference in Colossians (see later) which links festivals with Sabbaths in its discussion of 'days'. If Paul had meant to exclude the weekly Sabbath, we might have expected him to make such an important exception explicit.

Paul says that Christians are not to condemn the man who treats all days alike and regards them as being of equal importance. It is not a sin, Paul says to treat Sunday like a weekday, although Paul would surely have regarded adultery or coveting as sins. Although the Sabbath is in the Ten Commandments, Paul treats it differently from the other commandments. He does not seem to regard it as binding on conscience, but classifies it with other ceremonial provisions, like food and festivals, which were signs of the old covenant.

The situation confronting Christians in Rome differed in one important respect from the situation in Britain today. The Christians were a tiny minority. The laws of the land were in no way geared towards a Christian pattern of life. Thus, Paul argues, whether the individual makes the personal sacrifice necessary to keep one day of the week special is a matter for his individual conscience. In Britain, the Sunday trading laws confront Christians with a different problem. The present law does reflect Christian values of family and community life, and of the rhythm of life. The issue is not our *individual* decision as to whether to observe an outward ritual in a pagan society, but whether *as a society* it is important to maintain a social institution which in many ways reflects Christian values.

There are at least four ways in which our present Sunday pattern helps us to keep the principle of love for God and for our neighbour in our society.

1. The main principle or purpose lying behind the Sabbath law is that we should love the Lord our God with all our heart, mind, soul and strength (Luke 10:27). By making one day of the week special, we are helped to give the best of our time to God, rather than its fag-ends.

2. Following the principle behind the Sabbath law as stated in Deuteronomy, Sundays help us protect low-income workers from coming under pressure to work seven days a week.

3. Following one of the principles behind the law as it is stated in Exodus, Sundays help us preserve family, community and church life as they ensure everybody is off work at the same time, without which it is so much more difficult for family and friends to spend time together.

4. Following the creation ordinance, Sundays help to ensure everybody follows God's design of regular rest and a seven-day rhythm in life.

If Sundays are lost in Britain as a special day, all these principles could be observed by other means. For example, special laws could be passed to protect workers. New national holidays could be made to give more collective time off to the family. Another day could be set aside to give a seven-day rhythm to life but in practice this is most unlikely to happen. If we want to see the principles of Christian living followed in our society, and if we want to be able to follow them relatively easily in our personal lives, we should struggle to keep Sunday free of the competing claims of commercial activity.

GALATIANS 4:9-11

"But now that you know God - or rather are known by God - how is it that you are turning back to those weak and miserable principles? Do you wish to be enslaved by them all over again? You are observing special days and months and seasons and years! I fear for you, that somehow I have wasted my efforts on you."

COLOSSIANS 2:16

"Therefore do not let anyone judge you by what you eat or drink, or with regard to a religious festival, or a New Moon, or a Sabbath day. These are a shadow of the things that were to come; the reality, however, is found in Christ."

Jewish agitators had visited the churches in Galatia. They were trying to persuade Christians that to follow Christ required that they should adopt certain aspects of Jewish culture. Their primary target was to get Christians circumcised, but apparently they also aimed to impose the food laws and all the Jewish festivals, including the Sabbath. Paul insists that a Christian is no longer 'under the law'. God no longer imposes legal sanctions. Christians are free from the curse of the law, i.e. from its legal sanctions, as Christ bore the curse for us upon the Cross (Gal 3:13).

This is not to say that there are no longer any *rules* governing a Christian's behaviour, or that God does not punish evil among his children. When Paul tells the Ephesians to 'honour father and mother' (Eph 6:2), it is more than just good advice. Paul expected the command to be obeyed. When Christians in Corinth abused the Lord's Supper, and some became sick and died, Paul warned them that God was punishing them (1 Cor 11:29-30). So rules still help the Christian to please God, and obedience is still important.

However, this passage makes it clear that Paul does not regard the Sabbath, or any other day, as being one of those rules which must be obeyed. The Sabbath or Sunday may be helpful, but it is not always a part of Christian obedience. While Paul does not here (or anywhere else) throw out the idea of keeping a day special, and indeed the references in Acts and Corinthians suggest he kept a day special himself, Christians need not always be bound by it. It is not an absolute like other commands, such as those not to worship other gods and not to commit adultery. If we do not always keep Sunday special, we are not necessarily committing a sin. What matters is not outward observance of a day of the week, but obdedience to the commands of Jesus to love God and love our neighbour. To keep Sunday special is important because it is helpful in fulfilling those two fundamental obligations.

How we decide to use Sunday is not something we should take casually. Paul says to the Romans that everyone "should be fully convinced in his own mind" that he is doing the right thing. For most Christians this will mean making worship, bible-study, fellowship and time for other people the overriding priorities on Sunday. But people's circumstances vary. Take the case of a professional footballer. Suppose he sometimes has to play on Sundays to keep his place in the team. By being in a leading team he has opportunities to speak about his faith to other players, and to the fans - opportunities no-one else would have. Should he give up football in order to keep Sunday special? Paul would have said "It's up to you". He should follow his conscience. He must make sure that he makes time in the week to be with God and with God's people, to worship, to pray and to study. He must make sure his motives are right. However, if he chooses to miss Sunday church services to play football instead, and he does so for God's glory, that need not affect his relationship with God, and other Christians should not criticize him for it.

"Therefore, since the promise of entering his rest still stands, let us be careful that none of you be found to have fallen short of it. For we also have had the gospel preached to us, just as they did; but the message they heard was of no value to them, because those who heard did not combine it with faith. Now we who have believed enter that rest, just as God has said,

> *'So I declared on oath in my anger,*
> *"They shall never enter my rest." '*

And yet his work has been finished since the creation of the world. For somewhere he has spoken about the seventh day in these words: 'And on the seventh day God rested from all his work'. And again in the passage above he says, 'They shall never enter my rest'.

It still remains that some will enter that rest, and those who formerly had the gospel preached to them did not go in, because of their disobedience. Therefore God again set a certain day, calling it Today, when a long time later he spoke through David, as was said before:

> *'Today, if you hear his voice,*
> *do not harden your hearts.'*

For if Joshua had given them rest, God would not have spoken later about another day. There remains, then, a Sabbath-rest for the people of God; for anyone who enters God's rest also rests from his own work, just as God did from his. Let us, therefore, make every effort to enter that rest, so that no one will fall by following their example of disobedience."

In the letter to the Hebrews, the writer explores many of the ways in which the new covenant supersedes and is better than the old covenant. He is concerned to demonstrate especially to Jewish Christians in what ways the ceremonial law of the old covenant is fulfilled in the person and work of Jesus, the Messiah. The Sabbath issue is one of the themes he puts under this microscope, and it is the 'rest' idea which he focusses on in this passage.

God promised 'rest' right at the beginning, and yet the Old Testament writers repeatedly affirm that the Israelites, through disobedience, never obtained that rest. Moses and the Law had failed to give the people rest. Nor had the entry into the Promised Land under Joshua resulted in rest. Therefore, the writer of Hebrews argues the 'rest' must refer forward to something else, which is to be available for the people of God later. This rest is that which comes through salvation in Christ and is available now to any who cease from their own work, and trust in what God has done for them through Christ (cf Matt 11:28).

Why does the writer of Hebrews call it the "Sabbath-rest"? This is the only place where the word is found in the New Testament. As well as being a sign of the old covenant, the weekly Sabbath had been a sign of an eternal reality. This eternal rest, which was symbolized under the old covenant through the observance of a Sabbath, is now available through the new and 'better' covenant. A new people of God were to inherit it. So the fulfilment of the Sabbath law does not lie in another day of the week observed by the Christian, but in the salvation which God has given to his people through the Cross. The Sabbath rest is just a picture of that eternal salvation.

So is there any point in keeping one day special now? If the whole point of the Sabbath was to point forwards to the promise of eternal rest, why bother with keeping one day of the week special any more? No day today carries the theological significance of pointing forward to something which is to come. Our salvation is already here. So if we keep one day special today, we are doing something fundamentally different from keeping an Old Testament Sabbath. We are not keeping a God-ordained sign of our covenant, our relationship with God. We are not symbolizing a promise of God to provide rest to his people in the future. However we are giving the best of our time to God, we are helping to preserve family life, we are protecting low income workers, and we are proclaiming to society the importance we attach to the Resurrection. It is extremely valuable to keep a day special in this way, but since it is not a sign of the new covenant and is nowhere commanded in the New Testament, it remains a matter of individual conscience as to whether we observe it or not.

REVELATION 1:10

"On the Lord's Day, I was in the Spirit, and I heard behind me a loud voice like a trumpet . . ."

The only further reference to the Sabbath-Sunday issue is in the book of Revelation. This was written by the apostle John, right at the end of his life when the church was already undergoing fierce persecution. John does not set about a theological treatise on the issue. There is just a passing reference to "the Lord's Day" in the introduction to one of his visions. However, it does provide one or two important insights.

The Greek adjective used to express "Lord's" (of the Lord - in Greek - *kuriakos*) is only found in two places in the New Testament. It refers only to the Lord's Supper (I Cor 11:20) and the Lord's Day (Rev 1:10). The phrase may either mean the supper or day which the Lord instituted, or that which proclaims him. Either the first day of the week is the day the Lord instituted, or the day which proclaims him. The lack of evidence for the former suggests it is the latter. If so, Christians today should also seek to proclaim Christ through their use of his day.

This is the only reference to "the Lord's Day" in the New Testament. The only other reference to "the Lord's holy day" in the Bible comes in Isaiah's prophetic statements about the Sabbath (Is 58:13-14). The context of John's introduction to his visions is the Resurrection and the Lord's return, so John is probably referring to the first day of the week, the day of the Resurrection. If he is, this would suggest many in the early church thought of the first day of the week as in some sense special while the apostles were still alive. If the Lord's day was special to the apostle John and the early church, there is every reason why we should continue to regard it as special today.

4. THE ECONOMIC EFFECTS

The prospect of Sunday trading raises a range of economic issues. How many shops will find it worth while to open on Sundays? What will be the impact on sales, costs, prices and, perhaps most important, employment? What will be the impact on the retail sector and, particular, how will small retailers fare? The Home Office commissioned an independent economic review by the Institute for Fiscal Studies (IFS) and this was presented to the Auld Committee. Their review is the most thorough study available and what follows is based closely on their conclusions, with some small reservations. It emerges that the economic effects of Sunday trading might in fact be negative. In any event, the economic effects will be small.

1. HOW MUCH SUNDAY TRADING WILL TAKE PLACE?

Estimates of the likely extent of Sunday opening in England vary. On the basis of their model of the retail sector, the IFS estimate that shops accounting for 48 per cent of total turnover will open on Sundays (para 258). The number of shops which open, the Home Secretary believes, will be 20 to 30 per cent of all shops for most of the year.[4] He did not indicate how he reached this figure but it appears to be supported by the results of a survey carried out by the Business Studies Faculty at the Polytechnic of Central London, based on questionnaires answered by 40 leading retailers. They predicted that between 15 and 20 per cent of high street shopping centres will adopt Sunday opening together with all, or almost all, out-of-town centres, but that there will be widespread pre-Christmas, sales and holiday Sunday opening.[5]

Mr. Terry Burke who carried out the survey concluded that the "majority of high street multiples are cautious over opening".[6] There is a slight problem here. Any multiple which is eager to open on Sunday may also be eager to give the opposite impression in order to dispel the fears of those who do not want to see the traditional character of Sunday spoiled. That aside, Mr. Burke added that the high street multiples will only open "if they consider it likely to be profitable or *as a reaction to competitive pressures and fears of loss of market share*".[7] This is a crucial admission. Although Sunday opening may start at a relatively low level, the dictates of competition are likely to cause more and more shops to open. The John Lewis Partnership is of the view that

---

[4] House of Commons, Official Report, 20 May 1985, Vol 79, No. 120, Col. 756.

[5] Cited in the *Financial Times*, 29 May 1985: "Big Retailers Cool on Seven Day Week for Shoppers".

[6] ibid.

[7] ibid.

"Sunday opening would be progressive and irresistible".[8] In times of recession, particularly, shops may extend their opening hours in an attempt to maintain turnover. Once open for longer hours, there will be a ratchet effect and it will be much harder to reduce them again. John Lewis are not alone when they "expect that, in time, Sunday would become, in many places, the second busiest shopping day of the week".[9]

There is another important factor which will tend to generate additional Sunday opening. The IFS reached their figure of 48 per cent on the assumption that Sunday work would be paid at double time. However, as they say elsewhere, "if the premium were considerably less - say one-and-a-half times - then retailers would find Sunday opening more attractive . . ."[10] The double time premium is protected by the Wages Councils. These are soon to be reformed or abolished. One possible reform is to restrict them to establishing minimum rates of pay, removing their influence on premium rates. Under abolition, the Sunday premium would be left to market forces. If "left to market forces the size of the Sunday wage premium would probably fall".[11] Either way, as Sunday labour becomes cheaper, Sunday opening will steadily increase.

The experience in Scotland is often used to suggest that these estimates are exaggerated, especially the notion that Sunday could become the second busiest shopping day in many places. However, Scotland's experience, as we show in a later section and as the Auld Committee state, is not a reliable indication of likely events in England. A consideration of the economic factors which are relevant in England makes it clear that if Sunday trading is permitted it will take place sooner or later on a substantial scale.

2. SALES, COSTS AND PRICES

The volume of retail sales is unlikely to increase to any significant degree if seven-day trading starts. If retail turnover is to rise then either people must spend a higher proportion of their income, or a fixed amount of consumer expenditure must be directed in greater measure towards the retail sector. Economic research provides very little evidence to support the view that an extension in trading hours will increase total consumer expenditure (Appx 6 para 71). Given fixed expenditure, longer trading hours may cause some to be directed away from other items (e.g. package holidays and 'pub lunches') and on to retail goods, and spending by foreign tourists may rise slightly. However, the sums involved are small amounting to an extra one or two per cent of turnover at the outside (Appx 6 paras 72-74).

[8] Mr. I. Anderson, Director of Trading, John Lewis Partnership, as reported in *Drapers' Record*, 13 November 1982. Quoted in "The Choice Must be Hours", USDAW, February 1983, p.17.

[9] Evidence of John Lewis Partnership to Auld Committee, quoted in *The Gazette*, 21 January 1984, p. 1163.

[10] S. M. Jaffer and C. N. Morris, *Sunday Trading and Employment*, IFS, 1985.

[11] ibid., p. 12.

On the other hand, seven-day trading will raise costs to a significant degree in the short run. The IFS estimated that if a retailer opens for eight hours on Sunday, this will add nearly 22 per cent to his total labour costs (assuming the payment of double time) (Appx 6 para 67). The total costs for heating and lighting will also rise. Some retailers will find they have to open, since they would otherwise lose too large a proportion of their turnover. Whether they open or not, even once staffing arrangements have been adjusted to maximise labour productivity, "for retailers accounting for around 90 per cent of current sales, the medium term effect would be to increase costs per unit of sales" (Appx 6 para 109).

Faced with higher costs, but stable income, retailers will either find they have to accept reduced profit margins or raise their prices. The IFS believe the major part of the adjustment will be on profit margins. In practice, retailers will raise prices wherever they think that the market will bear such increases. Whenever this happens, both weekday and weekend shoppers, will have to pay for the additional convenience enjoyed by those who shop on Sundays.

In the long run, a period of ten years or more, the IFS suggests that costs in the retail trade might be 2 per cent lower than they would be in the absence of Sunday trading, largely owing to the extinction of less efficient retailers. If this were fully passed on in prices, this would lower the Retail Prices Index by 0.4 per cent. Even this small, once-for-all, reduction in prices cannot be guaranteed, however, because cost reductions will only be passed on in prices if the retail sector remains competitive. We suggest below that Sunday trading may adversely affect the competitive environment in the retail sector.

3. EMPLOYMENT

With unemployment levels as high as they are, the possibility of raising employment through Sunday trading has attractions. The IFS are at pains to stress that "the estimation of likely employment effects is extremely problematic, so that precise estimates are impossible to obtain".[12] On the basis of their model, however, they predict that Sunday opening would generate a demand for labour on Sunday "equivalent" to 73,000 full-time jobs.

They explain that this will be offset in two ways. In the short run, there will be a net loss in weekday jobs since sales on the other six days of the week will be reduced. In the long run, the physical volume of the retail sector will also have to fall. This is because Sunday trading will automatically increase the capacity of the retail sector, relative to the market for its services, since shopping opportunities will rise relative to expenditure. As the retail sector readjusts its capacity downwards, there will be a reduction in jobs.

[12] ibid., p. 18.

The overall effect on employment in the retail industry will depend upon the impact Sunday trading has on total sales. If there is no increase in sales, in the short run there would be a decrease of 5,000 full-time equivalent jobs, and in the long term a further 15,000 jobs. If there is a 2 per cent increase in sales, in the short run there would be an increase of 22,000 jobs, but in the long run only an increase of 9,000 jobs.[13] The original report by the IFS considered it necessary to look only at the case where there is no sales increase, and so predicted an eventual loss of 20,000 jobs. It was only in a second report, carried out under a grant from the Federation of Multiple DIY Retailers who are lobbying hard for unrestricted Sunday trading, that the more favourable sales increase cases were considered.

This is not the full story, however. Suppose there is an increase in expenditure on retail goods. It will come from one of two sources: either a fall in the volume of saving in which case fewer funds will be available for investment; or, as is more likely, it will be diverted from other forms of expenditure, in which case jobs will be lost in other areas of the economy. The IFS study did not include estimates of these job losses in other sectors. There is no prospect of significant job creation from Sunday trading. Indeed, there is reason to believe that in the long run, employment may fall.

4. THE CHANGING STRUCTURE OF THE RETAIL SECTOR

Sunday trading will introduce and accelerate a number of changes in the structure of the retail trade. In particular, small independent shops will be put in an unenviable position if high street shops and out-of-town shopping centres open on Sunday. Their market share will shrink as custom is drawn away elsewhere on Sunday. Competitive forces will therefore put them under considerable pressure to open seven days a week. This will be difficult for small shops, however, who cannot so readily staff a shop for seven days as a large multiple, particularly if skilled or experienced staff are needed. Many families owning businesses will be compelled to work seven days a week, and many small retailers will be driven out of business.

We consider later the social effects of this on pensioners, and others who find it hard to travel to the supermarket. Here we consider the economic impact of this trend. Multiple chain stores already dominate retailing, accounting for over half of total turnover, and in food retailing two-thirds of turnover.[14] The introduction of Sunday trading will increase this dominance, which may be a reason why a number are seeking deregulation. The retail sector is also at present fiercely competitive. The IFS is of the view that this competitive environment will not be jeopardized and may even be enhanced.

[13] ibid., Table 3.1, p. 10.

[14] Business Statistics Office, *Business Monitor, SDO 25, Retailing, 1982*, HMSO 1984.

However, there can be serious misgivings about this view. The Monopolies and Mergers Commission in their report on "Discounts to Retailers" (1981) commented: "The fact that no clear sign has yet appeared that the rate of growth in the market share of the largest multiple retail chains has begun to slacken suggests that retailing might come to be dominated by a few very large retailers to such an extent that competition would suffer and the consumer would be worse served than at present . . ."[15] It is not only consumers who stand to lose out. As Dr. Kirby of the University of Wales reminded the Auld Committee, the "increased decline in the independent sector would be damaging to the interests of the manufacturers and suppliers who, increasingly, would become dependent on the large retail organisation as outlets for their products".[16]

5. WHO WILL GAIN AND WHO WILL LOSE?

Overall, there are few economic benefits to be gained from Sunday opening. However, there will be gainers and losers. The DIY centres and garden centres in particular can anticipate substantial turnover on Sundays. Other retailers, however, will find they have to stay open for seven days instead of six to support the same level of turnover. Large retailers are better equipped to do this than independent retailers and will gain at their expense. Many small retailers will be driven out of business. The profit margins of some are already relatively slender and this makes them vulnerable to any increase in costs. For other self-employed retailers it will simply be physically difficult to stay open for seven days.

An obvious question to ask is why so many shops will open if so few will benefit. The reason is that when each individual retailer weighs up the cost of opening on Sunday against the loss of turnover if the shop stays shut, many will find it worthwhile to open. The first shop to open steals a march on his competitors. However, as more and more shops open, still on the basis of rational decisions by individual retailers, a position is reached, as the IFS notes, where it would in fact have been better for retailers as a whole to have stayed shut on Sunday (Appx 6 para 86). That is one of the ironies of the Sunday trading debate.

One other industry which might benefit somewhat from deregulation is the tourist industry, and shops in tourist areas. The English Tourist Board believe unrestricted trading would be a "small but significant improvement in the service we offer to tourists".[17] The gains will be marginal, however, in most

---

[15] Monopolies and Mergers Commission, "Discounts to Retailers", 1981, Chap 9, para 17.

[16] David A. Kirby, "Shops Act 1950: Restrictions on Trading", *Area* (1984), 16.3, p. 235.

[17] Evidence of English Tourist Board to the Auld Committee.

cases. It is difficult to conceive of many tourists attracted to England as a possible venue for their holiday but deciding against it because the shops are only open for six days a week.

Consumers will have greater choice over the times they go shopping, but this will be offset by a smaller choice of establishment. Furthermore, certain functions, such as restocking, cleaning premises and refurbishing, which at present can be carried out when stores are closed might need to be carried out whilst customers are in the store.

Our examination of the economic effects on Sunday trading has highlighted the fact that these might be negative in terms of prices, profits, employment and competition. There will be some retailers who gain, notably the DIY centres and garden centres, but others, notably independent traders, will lose. As with any other set of economic predictions, the precise figures must be treated as estimates and no more. Nonetheless, it is clear that, positive or negative, the economic effects of permitting Sunday trading will be relatively small. A case for or against Sunday trading is difficult to make on economic grounds. The real debate lies elsewhere.

5. THE SOCIAL IMPLICATIONS

The case against Sunday trading is built out of a concern for people and their way of life. The costs of Sunday trading will be borne in particular by a number of weaker groups in society. For a wide range of people the present special character of Sunday provides a variety of benefits which would steadily be lost. These social costs are examined one by one:

1. THE EFFECT ON THE FAMILY

The importance of the family is a theme which can be detected throughout the Bible. The family unit was established as normative at creation, and in the Ten Commandments the command to honour father and mother is given before the command not to murder. The family - and not the state, the courts, the company or the school - is the central social institution. As George Gilder suggests, there is a real sense in which every other form of human activity, including the business and the politics in society "finds its ultimate test in the quality of the home".[18]

By this test, the arrival of Sunday trading does not fare well. Its introduction will have an adverse effect on the family life of all those families where one member or another is called upon to work on Sunday. Such work, whether by father, mother or teenager, by definition, reduces the possibility of the members of the family doing things together. Such work will also break into "the nexus of relationships for which Sunday gives space". It will make "visiting, friendship and communal activities outside the home" more difficult.[19]

Some of the Sunday work in shops will be done by regular workers employed at other times during the week. At present, out of 2.2 million people employed in retailing, nearly half are married women. Up to a million married women, if asked to work on Sundays, will be under considerable pressure to work on the one day when their husbands are most likely to be at home and their children are off school. In a climate of high unemployment, this pressure will often amount to a choice between their families and their jobs. But in many cases, household financial commitments will have been made on the assumption of two incomes, and so many women will be all but forced to choose not their families but their jobs. This is bound to have an effect both on

---

[18] G. F. Gilder, *Sexual Suicide*, Millington, 1979, p. 244. Quoted in O. R. Johnston *Who Needs the Family?* Hodder and Stoughton 1979.

[19] British Council of Churches and Free Church Federal Council, "A Critique of the Auld Report", para 14.

marital relationships and children's welfare.

For family businesses the problem will be particularly acute. Many will face considerable competitive pressure to open on Sundays and, because suitable staff can be difficult or expensive to obtain, to man the shop seven days a week. Such businesses may be forced to choose between keeping one day for rest and family life, and staying in business.

Some of the Sunday work in shops will be done by teenagers. Saturday opening in shops attracts large numbers of teenagers as Saturday-only workers, and a similar set of Sunday-only, or weekend-only, workers seems likely. In some cases, this will provide a way for unemployed teenagers to begin to get work experience. However, there are also many possible negative repercussions. There is the possibility of exploitation through long hours at low rates of pay. For some teenagers, jobs over the weekend, on top of school or college during the week, will do little to help their well-being or education. Another effect of Sunday work by teenagers may be to widen the distance often felt between adults and adolescents. The family link between generations as well as between spouses will be weakened.

How many families will actually be affected in this way? This depends in the first instance on how many shopworkers are required to work on Sundays, and estimates vary. The IFS predicted that on any one Sunday 350,000 shopworkers will be needed (Appx 6 para 197). This figure is reached as follows. There are 2.2 million workers in retailing. On average, one million are at work at any one time during weekdays. To open shops accounting for just under half the retail sector's capacity would at first sight seem to need just under half a million workers. However, the IFS argue the figure will in fact be as low as 350,000. The shops which are likely to open would be those which use less labour than average since it will be relatively cheaper for these shops to open, and relatively few management and supervisory tasks would be done on Sundays. The estimate of the IFS then is probably a lower limit. If there is a rota system for Sunday work, as is quite likely, two, three or four times as many as 350,000 will find themselves involved in Sunday work at some time or another. We are already talking about up to a million or more families, but if Sunday opening is more widespread than the IFS anticipate, this base figure of 350,000 will be an underestimate.

Moreover, Sunday working will not be restricted to retailing. Workers will be needed in ancillary services such as public transport, waste disposal, police, traffic wardening, wholesale distribution, shop inspection, electricity and telephone servicing, banking and so on. The time span involved may be a number of years, but, as time goes on, it seems almost certain that more and more families will be affected.

The Auld Committee is at pains to stress a number of alleged advantages of Sunday trading to family life. They suggest that "some wives and mothers who are tied to the house with children all week may find relief in escaping to a different environment on a Sunday when their husbands are at home and able to spend some time with the children" (para 140).

The other side of the story, omitted by the Auld Committee, is not so attractive. Sunday work by husband or wife will mean that less time is available to a married couple for companionship and communication. A study by Elliot into the conflicts between work and family life in junior hospital doctors' families, where the problem arises from heavy workloads of doctors, sheds light on some of the problems which might arise when time together is reduced.[20] In a sample of 38 doctors' wives, "limitations on husband-wife interaction ... were reported by 71% ... this was for wives the most stressful consequence of heavy workloads - as indicated by the intensity as well as the frequency of their accounts of loneliness".[21] The married shopworkers will, of course, have companions at work but these relationships will rarely be more than superficial. Elliot's attempt to discern the depth of the emotional bond between husbands and wives found a weaker link for doctors than for dentists, whose lighter workloads allowed more time together.

The implications of this are unwelcome. It is in open, secure, caring relationships that many of our deepest human needs are met. Of course, keeping Sunday free from work does not guarantee such relationships. But Sunday work cannot possibly help them. The factors that lead up to divorce are various, but limited or deteriorating opportunities for companionship may often be an important contributory factor.

Sunday work by mother or father will mean that less time is available for them to be with their children. Consider the child, aged 5 to 11, who is at school during the daytime or weekdays, and goes to bed fairly early in the evening. If his mother goes out to work on Sunday there will be a significant reduction in the number of hours of contact and personal attention that the child will receive from her. The same will be true of attention from fathers, as Sunday work spreads from shops to ancillary services. There is an established body of evidence now that parental deprivation is associated with problems for children in their emotional development and long-term mental health.[22] However, it is not just the child who loses out. Elliot's study showed that overworked doctors who were fathers felt "that they were missing out on the pleasures of seeing their children grow up and were becoming 'shadowy' figures in the background of their lives."[23] The mother or father who finds he or she is often working on Sunday, may soon begin to feel a similar disappointment. There will rarely be a straight choice between job and family, but in almost every case, as work time encroaches on what has previously been time for family, a tension between the two will be felt more acutely, with frustrations, disappointment and emotional costs for all involved.

On a different tack, the Auld Committee suggest that "Sunday shopping

[20] Faith Robertson Elliot, "Professional and Family Conflicts in Hospital Medicine", *Social Sciences and Medicine*. Vol 13A, 1979, pp. 57-64.

[21] ibid.

[22] For example, John Bowlby, *Child Care and the Growth of Love*, Penguin 2nd edition, 1965.

[23] Robertson Elliott, 1979 p. 61.

has much to offer the family . . ." (para 135). They go on, ". . . many find that Saturday is not a good day for the kind of shopping that involves the whole family, for household goods, things for the garden, presents and clothes. It is often only on Sundays that they can all get together to make shopping outings of that sort. It must be good for them to be able to spend time together in a leisurely and relaxed way, discussing projects and purchases of interest to them all" (para 136).

The Auld Committee appear to have a romanticised vision of the family shopping outing which bears more resemblance to a television commercial than the reality. In the first place, just how many purchases "involve the whole family", parents and children? If the family are in a shop on Sunday, it is unlikely that the children are there to be consulted. They are generally there because they cannot be left at home. Rather than having to tag along in the shops, they would probably prefer an outing, or the attention of their parents at home. The notion that Sunday shopping is "leisurely and relaxed" is based on the fact that at present very few shops open, and those that do are uncrowded. But unrestricted Sunday trading will almost certainly lead to crowded shops. In many places it may become the second busiest shopping day so that Sunday shopping becomes less of a pleasure and more of struggle. The final irony is that as more people find themselves drawn into Sunday work, there will be that many fewer families with all their members free to go on these shopping outings in any case.

The Report also points to the fact that a "growing number of people live alone, many of them without or far from families. For them, and for families too sometimes, 'the traditional Sunday' can be a boring, lonely day. The opportunity to shop or work in a shop, or simply to see some life in the shopping high street, may offer a real improvement to the day" (para 138). The opportunity to shop, they do not mention, will also mean that other single people, above all elderly relatives, will not be visited because the would-be visitors will be shopping. The point that the Auld Committee fail to recognise is that, while "shopping on Sunday" may take some people's minds off their loneliness, it is at best a short-term palliative for a minority. The underlying effect will be to add yet another pressure on family cohesion, strengthening the very processes which make for lonely people in society.

For many, this idea of Sunday as the family day may still seem a well-meaning but vague and ungrounded generalisation. Yet there is both survey evidence and historical evidence to support the claim. The survey evidence is provided by Young and Wilmott who found, in Greater London, that 52% of shift workers and 34% of weekend workers said that work interfered with home and family, while only 27% of other workers did. They also found that men spend nearly 40% more time at home on Sundays than on weekdays, and that 9.5 hours were spent with the immediate family on a Sunday compared with 5.7 hours on weekdays.[24]

The historical evidence is provided by the USSR. In pursuit of "continuous

[24] M. Young and P. Wilmott, *The Symmetrical Family*, Routledge and Kegan Paul, 1973; Penguin Books, 1975.

production" between 1929 and 1940, various ways of staggering rest days so that machinery never stood idle were attempted. The number of rest days allowed was greater than the fifty-two the workers had when Sunday was their rest day. Nonetheless, the "experiment . . . was both unpopular and unsuccessful: families complained that they could not spend their rest days together - 'What do we have families for?' wrote a group of Moscow workers to *Pravda* in October 1929". In the end, the "seven-day week, with the rest day on Sunday, as is normal in most other countries, was therefore restored in the USSR: and there has been no further recurrence of exotic experiments".[25]

In the end, the real thrust of the family argument is this. We live in a society where the pressures on family life are greater than they have ever been before. One statistic after another documents the results of those pressures. In the twenty years from 1961 - 1980, the divorce rate rose 500%, so that one in three marriages now end in divorce.[26] Divorce produces one-parent families. An estimated 890,000 existed in 1980, and one and a half million children lived in such families.[27] As for children born today, as many as one in five will have parents who divorce before they are 16 years old.[28] The psychological harm on children affected by lack of parental attention and the emotional pain imposed on rejected spouses is often deep and enduring. Hundreds of thousands of people are struggling under it already. Whatever else we do with our law, the last thing we should do is allow it to impose yet another pressure on family life.

2. THE EFFECT ON SHOPWORKERS

This is a major issue in the Sunday trading debate and occupied almost the entire speech of the Shadow Home Secretary when the Auld Report and the Government's intentions were considered in the House of Commons. The welfare of shopworkers is inextricably bound up with any decision about trading on Sunday. Concern exists on two accounts. There is, first, the specific question of whether Sunday work will be voluntary or not. There are, in addition, fears that the Goverment may introduce legislation in a form which provides insufficient protection for shopworkers, with the result that their pay and conditions of work will fall in some instances to unacceptably low levels.

1. On the question of whether Sunday work should be voluntary, the Report concedes that "while some people are obviously happy to work on Sundays, others are not" (para 156), that there might be difficulty in getting sufficient

---

[25] Study Commission on the Family, *Families in the Future: a Policy Agenda for the '80s*, 1983, p. 11.

[27] ibid. p. 13.

[28] ibid. p. 12.

volunteers and that pressure might be applied on unwilling employees, with refusal to work on Sundays leading to dismissal or prejudiced promotion prospects (para 158-160).

The majority of submissions to the Committee which addressed the subject urged that Sunday working should be voluntary, and its voluntary character be protected in law. This was true of the general public as well. The National Consumer Council, who are strongly in favour of deregulation, noted of their surveys that "Respondents felt very strongly that staff should not be forced to work on Sunday . . ."[29] As USDAW put it "All days of rest are not equivalent and anyone who needs or is required to work on Sundays is bound to suffer socially".[30] Others rightly added that it is especially important that those with disinclination to work on Sundays on religious grounds be respected.

The Home Secretary has said that he "will look sympathetically at the best way of ensuring that established shopworkers cannot be compelled to work on Sundays".[31] This is not a commitment to make Sunday work voluntary, merely to look "sympathetically" at ways of doing this. The Auld Committee felt 'sympathy' for many of the views expressed by those who argued for continued regulation of trading hours but this did not prevent them from recommending abolition. The statement applies only to *established* shopworkers. It is not considered necessary to make Sunday work voluntary for new entrants into the retail sector. This will mean that if an applicant for a post as a shop assistant expresses any reservations about Sunday work, out of commitment to his family or his faith, he will probably be passed over in favour of someone else. We are in effect preparing to open the door to religious discrimination against committed Christians who firmly believe they should not work on Sunday.

When the Auld Committee considered the issue, having cited the oral evidence of a Bishop of the Church of England, they concluded that "a statutory provision specifically protecting shopworkers from being required to work against their will on Sundays . . . would be impracticable" (para 294). The Committee suggested, rather lamely, that "the provisons governing unfair dismissal in the Employment Protection (Consolidation) Act 1978 would in certain cases provide a safeguard" (para 282).

Some have argued that the whole question of a statutory provision to make Sunday work voluntary is a red herring because there will be an ample supply of volunteers. Such a view is too optimistic. The House of Fraser, which has opened in Scotland on one or more Sundays before Christmas, "has recently found the numbers of volunteers diminishing despite the relatively high pay levels" (para 156). Some leading retailers in favour of deregulation have stated that they do not wish to pressurize employees into Sunday work against

---

[29] Evidence of the National Consumer Council to the Auld Committee, para 66, p. 21.

[30] Union of Shop, Distributive and Allied Workers, "The Choice Must be Hours", Report on Shops Legislation, February, 1983, p. 21.

[31] House of Commons, Official Report, 20 May 1985, Vol. 79, No. 120, col. 756.

their wishes, but the experience of the House of Fraser suggests that this may be difficult to achieve in practice. Moreover, if Sunday trading becomes the norm, then the premium for Sunday work will fall, and the supply of willing labour will be reduced further. The more Sunday trading there is, the harder it will be to get a sufficient supply of 'volunteers'.

We need to decide whether a statutory provision would, in fact, be impracticable. In Massachusetts, where Sunday afternoon trading was permitted in 1983, the legislation which was introduced included the clause:

"No employee . . . shall be required to perform such [Sunday] work, and refusal to work for any retail establishment on Sunday shall not be grounds for discrimination, dismissal, discharge, reduction in hours, or any other penalty" (para 280).

So, the legislators in Massachusetts did not regard a statutory provision as impracticable, it would seem.

However, there is another side to the story. The Auld Committee suggests that "this provision has not yet been tested," because ". . . with the establishment of premium pay rates for Sunday working in shops . . . so far, there has been no difficulty in finding volunteers. It is difficult to say how effective the provision will be if . . . it is put to the test" (para 280). One does not have to agree entirely with this description of events in Massachusetts to realise that, in practice, any 'conscience clause' will be difficult to enforce. An employer has a range of sanctions at his disposal, some overt, some operating behind the scenes. Any employer suspected of discriminating against an employee because of his stand on Sunday work will always be able to claim that his actions were the result of some other factor. Even if machinery is set up to investigate disputes it will always be difficult to gather hard evidence of discrimination. As a result many employees may be unwilling to run the risk of trying to make use of any 'conscience clause'.

The 'conscience clause' is beleaguered by another problem. If, as we believe, a substantial number of shopworkers would prefer not to work on Sunday, then any person who exercises a conscience clause is imposing that much more Sunday work on his already reluctant colleagues. A 'conscience clause', far from ensuring the freedom of shopworkers to do as they please on Sunday, places many in a painful dilemma. Either they must forgo their personal principles and family responsibilities or else they must impose additional strains on their colleagues. It is weaknesses, and dilemmas, of this sort which mean that any clause to make Sunday work voluntary might in the end prove to be all but a dead letter.

To draw a few strands together, suppose for a moment that a statutory provision of this sort would be enforceable. If so, then it is nonsense to argue, as those in favour of abolition do, that a law against Sunday trading is unenforceable. The enforcement difficulties associated with ensuring that Sunday work is never 'compulsory' are considerably greater than those associated with ensuring shops do not open illegally. If, on the other hand, it would prove impossible to ensure that Sunday work is voluntary, then the additional convenience of longer opening hours, and the increased profits of a few retail chains, are bought at a high price. This price is the onerous conditions of employment which many shopworkers may be forced to accept if they wish to keep their jobs.

The conclusion that emerges is this. If there is a limited amount of Sunday trading, as is currently the case, then it is possible to employ well-paid volunteers. However, if Sunday trading arrives on a substantial scale, then it will be difficult to enforce any law making Sunday work voluntary, and this will matter because it will also be harder to find enough willing volunteers to staff the shops. Many believe, as the Crathorne Committee of 1964 did, that "the special character of Sunday ought to be preserved as far as practicable as a day of leisure in which a person is not required to pursue his weekday work and is free to do as he chooses".[32] If we really want Sunday work to remain voluntary, then Sunday trading must be restricted. If we are not concerned to keep it voluntary, we are acquiescing in a deliberate step which reduces the freedom of hundreds of thousands to make their faith, or their family, their first priority.

2. The second area of concern for shopworkers is that legislation could be passed in such a form that some shopworkers are subjected to intolerable conditions of work and rates of pay. This is a distinct issue from Sunday trading. However, there is overlap, and the same Act of Parliament will be relevant to both. Shopworkers are not a well-paid, advantaged group. Female shopworkers earn slightly over half the national average for women, and male shopworkers little more than a third of the national average for men. Although they make up one in eleven of the working population, they lack the trades union protection enjoyed by most other workers.

At present, they receive protection in law from two main sources: Part II of the Shops Act 1950 and the Wages Councils. Following the recommendation of the Auld Report, the Government will almost certainly repeal the Shops Act 1950 on the grounds that its provisions are too rigid to meet modern day requirements, and that most of the special provisions for young people are duplicated in other legislation. However, not all the provisions for young persons are duplicated elsewhere. Similar protection is not afforded elsewhere regarding the number of Sundays in a month for which young persons may be employed, and the number of weeks in a year for which an employer may engage young persons in overtime work (para 286). There has been no guarantee that a clause to ensure this protection will be added to existing legislation in other Acts. Leading retailers in favour of deregulation have in fact said there is no need to repeal the provisions of the Shops Acts relating to the maximum hours of employment of young people.

The chief area for concern is over the Wages Councils. These lay down minimum pay levels, rates of pay for overtime, weekends and bank holiday working, and minimum holiday requirements. The Auld Committee strongly

---

[32] Home Office, "Report of the Departmental Committee on the Law on Sunday Observance", (Chairman, Lord Crathorne), Cmnd 2528, HMSO, December 1964.

urged their retention, backed up by an adequately staffed Inspectorate to enforce their Orders. The Government have not yet reached a decision on their future, but have promised to do so before bringing forward legislation on the Shops Act. Many Government ministers favour their abolition as necessary to the development of a free economy and in the hope that this will increase employment. The House of Commons Select Committee on employment favoured their retention and reported that: "Ministers did not give an estimate of the increase in the number of jobs which might be expected to result from abolition. When pressed to do so in respect of young people, they were unable to: the message was 'try it out and see' ".[33]

Wages Councils at present provide protection for 2.7 million of Britain's lowest paid workers. However, there is a possibility that Wages Councils will go. If they do, the Auld Committee expressed the view that:

> "there would be strong likelihood of exploitation of some shopworkers in the form of lower wages, particularly for unsociable hours of work, and possibly in a longer working week. No doubt most good employers would continue to pay the established rates, but in the rapidly changing and uncertain conditions that might follow de-regulation of shop opening hours, if our recommendations were to be adopted, we cannot be sure that all employers would do so" (para 288).

Even where employers want to pay the established rates, there is a danger that: ". . . when you have no organisation, no parity of bargaining, the good employer is undercut by the bad, and the bad employer is undercut by the worst".[34] It was for this reason that Wages Councils were first introduced.

This issue of protection is distinct from that of Sunday trading, but there is significant overlap and the Shops Act 1950 dealt with both. In some retail outlets, demands will be placed on shopworkers to work on six or seven days of the week. Overall though, as employers streamline their use of labour in response to the new situation, the impact of Sunday trading will be to increase the proportion of part-time workers in retailing (para 267). Part-time jobs have their advantages. But they also have disadvantages because the conditions of employment of part-time workers tend to be worse than those of full-time employees. At less than sixteen hours work in a week, the workers fall outside the Employment Protection legislation. The average hourly wage of part-time workers in retailing is about two-thirds that of full-time workers. The TUC urged that, above all, we "must be wary of inadvertently sanctioning the growth of a new class of low paid and unprotected workers".[35]

The IFS predicted that aggregate earnings in the retail sector will rise, and some have argued that Sunday work will provide an opportunity for those on low incomes to supplement their weekly earnings, since Sunday work will be

[33] *The Times*, 17 May 1985, "MPs Say Wages Councils Should Not Be Abolished".

[34] House of Commons, Official Report, 28 April 1909, Vol. 4, Col. 388.

[35] Evidence of TUC to Auld Committee, para 18, p. 7.

paid at premium rates. But this overlooks the fact that, if Sunday work becomes the norm, and rates of pay are left to market forces, then the size of the Sunday premium will almost certainly fall, and might even disappear eventually.

Even though shopworkers receive protection in law at present there are cases of exploitation. The Shadow Home Secretary cited examples uncovered by the Low Pay Unit including one woman, a manageress of a dry cleaners, who works a $38\frac{1}{2}$ hour week and at the age of 23 receives only £44.56 gross.[36] If Sunday trading arrives, shopworkers will need not just the same level of protection they receive now, but considerably more. Although not its primary focus, the law against Sunday trading has served as a form of protection for shopworkers directly in terms of hours of work, and indirectly in terms of rates of pay. Since other protection is unlikely to be made available, another important reason for restricting Sunday trading is to protect low income shopworkers.

3. THE EFFECT ON SMALL SHOPKEEPERS AND PENSIONER HOUSEHOLDS

Sunday trading is usually presented as being of benefit to consumers and traders because of the increased freedom and flexibility it will allow for shopping times. There is another side to the story. Retail outlets will be open for longer, but since the turnover available to support retail enterprises will barely rise at all, the number of outlets is likely to decline. As the IFS pointed out, "longer opening hours would be likely to lead to some acceleration of the trend towards the disappearance from the market place of independent traders . . ." (Appx 6 para 15). A major difficulty for the independent trader is that he is often the only person who can act as manager or book-keeper. If a supermarket opens seven days a week, the managerial tasks can be shared out, but if a small shop is to open seven days then the owner-manager is virtually compelled to work seven days a week. It is not surprising, therefore, that a recent survey carried out by the Association of Independent Retailers found that 83% of small traders were opposed to the removal of all restrictions, and 62% believed that the present restrictions on Sunday trading should stay.[37]

However, it is not just independent traders who will suffer. In turn, consumers and communities will lose out. The small, local store performs a key role even in the most modern, efficient and concentrated retail sector. They provide a minor but useful service for the majority of consumers who use them for 'topping-up' purchases, for forgotten and emergency items and

---

[36] House of Commons, Official Report, 20 May 1985, Vol. 70, No. 120, Col. 397.

[37] Association of Independent Retailers, "Britain's Small Shopkeepers have given a Massive Thumbs Down to the Government's Suggestion of Unrestricted Trading", circular issued on 22 March 1985.

for perishable goods. Their role for a certain section of the consumer public is far more valuable. They meet many of the needs of the aged, the infirm, and the immobile who find it hard to travel to a supermarket in town and who often lack the resources to buy in bulk. The personal attention the small shopkeeper can provide is often particularly appreciated by the elderly. In a study in Watford, L. F. Daws and A. J. Bruce (1971) discovered that a decline in the provision of local shops would cause hardship to 90% of all pensioner households and 70% of all socio-economic groups.[38]

Communities in rural and urban areas may also be harmed. In rural areas, the arrival of Sunday trading will accelerate the demise of the village shop. In urban areas, it will cause some trade to swing away from the community centres in the towns and cities and out to out-of-town areas. In this way, one element in the "mutually supporting structures of urban life" would be undermined.[39]

These trends, the demise of the local shop and the growth of out-of-town shopping centres, are already occurring. However, Sunday trading will accelerate them. It has been suggested that since these things are happening anyway there is no point in retaining restrictions on Sunday trading. The argument is a *non sequitur*. We are faced with a choice. We know that if Sunday trading is permitted, some shopkeepers, consumers and communities will be harmed. If we retain restrictions, that harm will be forestalled, and we will have a breathing space in which to consider how to protect some of these interests.

4. THE EFFECT ON RESIDENTS NEAR SHOPPING CENTRES

As the Report itself says, "those who live in or near busy shopping areas would lose what little respite they have from the noise and bustle of the week" and "there is no doubt that many would be deeply upset by the change in their lives" (para 170). In fact, along with shopworkers, those who live near shopping centres are one of the two groups of people the Auld Committee singles out for special concern (para 272). They "reluctantly concluded that no special, practicable, legal protection can be devised" (para 293). The irony is that they may even have to pay for the privilege of shops disturbing what is now their one day of quiet. Sunday trading will require a range of services to be provided by the local authorities on Sundays (e.g. shop inspectors, waste disposal). This may raise expenditure, and if so, their rates are likely to rise too. Another group, those who live beside main roads, will be affected

---

[38] L. F. Daws and A. J. Bruce. *Shopping in Watford*. Garston. 1971.

[39] Evidence of John Lewis Partnership to the Auld Committee. See *The Gazette*, 21 January 1984, p. 1163.

similarly as traffic volumes increase. When deliveries of stock start to take place on Sundays, for fresh foodstuffs for example, there will be heavy lorries in the traffic.

Retailers' and consumers' organisations exist to express their view on Sunday trading. There is even pressure on behalf of tourists and the tourist industry for seven day trading. Yet no lobby exists to represent the views of the people whose 'quality of life' will be reduced by the traffic and disturbance which Sunday trading will bring in its wake.

5. THE IMPACT ON ALCOHOL CONSUMPTION

If the Auld Committee's recommendations are carried out, then alcohol will be freely available in retail outlets at all hours and on all days. In theory, this will not be so different from the existing situation since alcohol can be bought in shops on weekdays and Sundays until 8.00 pm. However, the volume of sales on Sunday will rise as the number of people out shopping increases. The extension of trading hours from 8.00 pm to midnight will mean that alcohol is available in shops at times when previously it was not available at all, or only in licensed premises. Once this happens, the principle of fair competition will make a relaxation of the licensing hours all but irresistible.

Alcohol consumption is a major contributory factor to fatal road accidents and violent crimes,[40] not to mention all the personal and family problems it can cause. As the *British Medical Journal* stated in May 1982: "If we are to have fewer alcohol problems, then we as a nation must drink less."[41] It is ironic though that a Goverment which favours liberalisation of licensing hours has felt driven by football hooliganism to announce a forthcoming Bill to ban possession of alcohol at football grounds and on football coaches. Clearly, the length of opening hours is far from the only factor leading to alcohol abuse, but it is probably a factor in the equation. If we want to continue to limit the times when alcohol can be purchased, then it will be important to continue to control trading hours.

6. THE IMPLICATIONS FOR OUR DEMOCRACY

The manner in which the Government is handling the Sunday trading issue gives some cause for concern. Most obvious is the fact that they have made

---

[40] See Department of Environment, "Report of Departmental Committee of Drinking and Driving" (The Blennerhassett Report), HMSO, 1976; and Rt. Revd. Timothy Dudley Smith, "Alcohol and the Witness of the Church", speech presented to Norwich Diocesan Synod, 12 June 1982.

[41] *British Medical Journal*, May 1982, quoted in Dudley Smith, "Alcohol and the Witness of the Church", 1982.

deregulation party policy. In the debate in May 1985, Conservative MPs were put under considerable pressure to support the Government, as a three-line Whip was applied. On every occasion to date when reform of the Shops Act has been considered by Parliament, there has been a free vote, not least because attitudes towards Sunday can properly be regarded as a question of conscience. Only two years ago in 1983, the Under-Secretary of State for the Home Department said:

> "There are important considerations and fears about the character of Sunday . . . These fears are held in many parts of the House and I agree that they are an important factor. That is why the Government adhere to the view, which successive Governments have adhered to, that the decision must be for the individual conscience of hon. Members."[42]

The Government appears to have changed its mind.

Some Conservative MPs objected to Sunday trading strongly enough to vote against their party and some abstained, but there were others who were somewhat unhappy with the proposals, but felt obliged to support the Government. An important feature of our democratic tradition has been that on issues like these MPs are free to honour their personal moral convictons, and, in the case of Christians, to respect an authority higher than that of the Government. It is a disturbing thought that a number of MPs were placed in a dilemma of conscience, which for some probably felt like pressure to stifle their conscience.

Less widely publicised, but also disturbing, is the fact that the Conservative Party never announced an intention to remove restrictions on trading hours in its manifesto. The Government, therefore, is about to introduce a major social change without having informed the electorate beforehand, or receiving a mandate from them. There are a number of churchgoers, perhaps a large number, who voted Conservative who now feel betrayed. They feel strongly enough about the subject that had they known this would happen they would have voted for another party. To cap it all, the Prime Minister said in her foreword to the manifesto that "the most vital decision" facing the people at the election was "how to defend Britain's traditional liberties and distinctive way of life". It is precisely these "traditional liberties" and our "distinctive way of life" which are now being put at risk.

There is a still wider issue. If a law which removes restrictions on Sunday trading is enacted, it will have profound symbolic significance. For the last three centuries or more, legislation to keep Sunday largely free of commercial activity has been closely associated with deference to Christian precepts. If deregulation occurs, this will indicate in a visible way that Parliament is no longer concerned to base legislation on Christian principles. But as Bishop Desmond Tutu asked: "If God's writ does not run in the political sphere, then whose does?"

---

[42] House of Commons, Official Report, 4 February 1983, Vol 36, Col. 557.

7. WHAT ABOUT SCOTLAND?

The social arguments against Sunday trading form an impressive catalogue. However, many are not convinced. They point to Scotland, which is not covered by the Shops Act 1950, and its experience of Sunday trading. According to a recent MORI survey, only 16% of shops open on Sunday in Scotland, and 98% of individuals say they have not been personally inconvenienced by Sunday trading. They argue that this is clear evidence that deregulation will not affect the traditional character of Sunday much and that the social costs are minimal.

The comparison between Scotland and England, however, is open to many questions. There is greater built-in resistance to Sunday trading on religious and cultural grounds in Scotland. One reason why the 1950 Act was not extended to Scotland was that it was felt the churches and the weight of public opinion would be sufficient deterrent. Even now, church membership in Scotland runs at 37% of the adult population compared with 13% in England.[43] In addition, local authorities in Scotland at the time had the power to enact byelaws to prevent shop opening in Scotland if public opinion at the local level was against it.

Many Scottish shops have head offices in England where the management is geared towards six day opening and therefore operates on the same basis in Scotland. Discussion of deregulation of opening hours in England has already prompted a new look at Sunday trading in Scotland. A lower population density, and a large proportion of households without cars, have also made Sunday trading less attractive as they reduce the likely level of custom, particularly in out-of-town sites.

All these factors suggest that Sunday trading will be more widespread in England and the predictions of economic surveys and models suggest the same. The social costs will be correspondingly higher too. The threshold at which shopworkers are put under compulsion to work on Sunday has barely been reached in Scotland, for instance, but would be reached much sooner in England. The environmental impact, not only greater under a larger volume of trading, will also be more noticeable in densely populated and urbanised England.

It is no surprise, therefore, that the Auld Report states: "Our overriding conclusion from our review of the experience of other countries [including Scotland] is that their economic, social and historical traditions vary so much that none could provide a reliable guide" to what would happen in England (para 248)

[43] HMSO, *Social Trends No. 15*, London, 1985, p. 163.

8. THE IMPACT ON CHURCH LIFE

Churchgoers are not an insignificant proportion of the population and, as such, are an interest group whose views should be considered. Figures in *Social Trends* estimate that in 1985 there are 7.3 million adult members of Christian churches.[44] This amounts to 16% of the UK adult population.[45] A more recent national survey by MORI cited in the *Financial Times* found that 20% had been to church in the previous month.[46]

Church life, however, will be impaired by unrestricted Sunday trading in four tangible ways:

(a) *The church's congregation will be fragmented.* Some people who would like to attend the main service of the week or on Sunday morning will be unable to do so because they will be required to work. It will be much harder for the church family in any one area to gather together as a whole. On every day, some of the church members will be at work.

(b) *Church attendance will be made more difficult.* Many of those who are not required to work on Sundays will find it more difficult to get to church simply because it will be harder to find parking space. Others will opt to use Sunday mornings for shopping when previously they would have chosen to go to church. From one point of view, they are being given the choice, and choose not to go to church, and that opportunity to choose should be given to them. From another point of view, those people who benefit from their Christian faith, but who for one reason or another find their faith is often a quiet voice rather than a strident claim on their lives, will be faced with one more obstacle to the nurture of their faith.

(c) *Church worship, in some areas, will suffer.* Churches and church halls in towns and cities have been built and located on the assumption of a quiet Sunday. In those near shopping centres, the noise of traffic and the general activity will disturb services. It will be harder to pray, to contemplate, to worship quietly or to concentrate on the sermon.

(d) *The church of tomorrow will be weakened.* After Sunday trading is introduced, it will probably become rarer for an individual to be introduced into church life, where he might find the opportunity to grow into Christian faith. Work and shopping will compete for his time, distract his attention and make the first step of pausing to consider the Christian faith harder to take.

Today we are a 'multi-cultural, multi-racial society'. Political and religious minorities should be accepted in the community and protected by law. It would be proper, for instance, to take the exemption which allows Jews to open on Sunday if they close on Saturday, and extend it to Moslems who close on Friday. However, the phrase, 'multi-cultural, multi-racial society' can

[44] HMSO, *Social Trends No. 15*, 1985. Adult membership of Trinitarian churches (projected figure for 1985). Table 11.8, p. 163.

[45] ibid.

[46] *Financial Times*, 9 April 1985: "Gardening Tops Sunday Survey".

often be exploited as a useful slogan. As the British Evangelical Council observes, it is important "to distinguish between those genuinely concerned for the welfare of minority ethnic groups and those who might appear to be using those groups as a lever to prise openings in legislation so that the juggernauts of their own retail businesses might drive through".[47]

The phrase, 'multi-cultural society' can be misleading because it suggests to some that there are many different cultural groups of roughly the same size. However, according to a poll conducted under the auspices of the Bible Society in 1983, some 84% of people in England consider themselves to be affiliated to a Christian church.[48] Many still want to be baptised, married and buried in church. This indicates where the religious and cultural sympathies of the vast majority lie. We must respect the traditions of others, but these should not be used as an excuse to sweep away our own values, including our tradition of Sunday as a special day.

9. THE RHYTHM OF LIFE

For many people, the most important feature of Sunday is that it is a day different from the rest. This difference is widely appreciated. With or without religious convictions, many people are grateful of a decisive break once each week in the routine of life. It affords relief from the pressures of the other six days, and it also provides positive opportunities for recreation and family life. Seven day trading would put this special character of Sunday in jeopardy. As the Report says, "widespread opening of shops on Sundays would affect the traditional character of the day very much more profoundly than the opening of cinemas, concert halls and theatres, or the holding of sporting events. The change . . . would have a significant effect on the feel of the day" (para 132). What at present is a different, more leisurely, day would steadily become much the same as all the others. The rhythm of life, the built-in balance of work and rest will give way to a random lack of pattern in the week. One person will have Tuesday and Wednesday off, another will have Monday and Friday off, and so on. Still more though, variation in the week will give way to monotony. There will be no single day in the week without work, without commerce, without hectic activity. The decision to allow unrestricted Sunday trading will not be an experiment. Once Sunday is lost, it will be almost impossible to recover.

---

[47] British Evangelical Council evidence to the Auld Committee, p. 3.

[48] Jan Harrison, "Attitudes to Bible, God, Church", Research Report, The Bible Society, June 1983, p. 9.

6.   THE LEGAL ARGUMENTS

Much of the desire for change springs from a widespread belief that the Shops Act 1950 is an out-of-date, ill-drafted and unworkable piece of legislation. The case for reform of some kind is not difficult to argue. The question is whether this reform has to take the form of total abolition of restrictions. We examine the various legal arguments in turn:

1. THE LAW IS FULL OF ANOMALIES AND COMPLICATIONS

There certainly are anomalies. This is not surprising in a piece of legislation which draws up a list of exemptions in a piecemeal fashion, some of which were on the statute book before the First World War (para 21). Thus it is legal to sell fish and chips on a Sunday provided they are not sold from a fish and chip shop, to sell gin but not dried milk, a pornographic magazine but not a Bible.

No one defends the existence of anomalies but it is absurd to use them as an argument for abolition of the law. To be sure anomalies provide an easy way of scoring points in the debate by making the opponent look ridiculous. But debating points are insubstantial things, readily turned on their head. One can buy a pornographic magazine but not a Bible, we are told. Does this mean we are to believe there are people writing to their MPs complaining that when they last went shopping on Sunday they were able to buy the pornographic magazine they wanted but had been disappointed when the shopkeeper told them they were not allowed to buy a Bible too!

Anomolies exist elsewhere. The sale of a take away cup of coffee hot is subject to VAT, but the sale of the same cup cold is not. It has never been suggested that this is a reason for abolishing VAT. Above all, though, the existence of anomalies is not an argument for abolition because they fall into insignificance when compared with the social costs which unrestricted Sunday trading will bring. An obsession with the tidiness of the law is petty when the issues at stake involve the welfare of many people.

Many anomalies can be tidied up. Some suggest a piecemeal approach, making more adjustments to the current schedule of exempt goods. For instance, where Chinese take-aways may sell fish and chips but fish and chip shops may not, the appropriate answer is to let fish and chip shops sell them too. It is not necessary to abolish all restrictions to achieve that. A still more effective way of removing anomalies probably lies in opting for a new form of exemption by type of shop or size of shop, rather than keeping solely to a list of exempt goods. Both of these approaches overcome the problem that many shops, under the present system, stock some exempt goods and some non-exempt goods.

The Auld Report describes the Act as "not easy for a lawyer to understand and interpret, let alone the average shopkeeper" (para 23). This might be said of a number of laws, notably UK tax law. Moreover, it is a statement which must be put in context. There are many situations where the law is straightforward. If a high street shop opens on Sunday with the intention of selling goods not listed as exempt in Schedule Five, and such a good is sold in exchange for money on that day, then it is quite clear that the law has been broken.

Nonetheless, there are complications. The system of exemption by type of good has led, for instance, to a situation where a chemist must decide that a buyer wants a pair of sunglasses for medical purposes to be sure that he is within the law to sell them on Sundays. Much ambiguous, even unhelpful, case law has arisen because the precise meaning of fundamental words like "retail", "wholesale", "shop", "serving", "viewing" and "place" was either poorly defined or not made clear at all. The lawyers and judges have sometimes had to work from almost incidental phrases in the text.

To sum up, the anomalies that exist are only an argument for removing or at least reducing them. Likewise, complications are only an argument for clarification and rationalisation of the law. Neither is an argument for its abolition. The case for that, if it exists, must lie elsewhere.

2. THE LAW IS OPENLY DEFIED BY SHOPKEEPERS ALREADY

If a law cannot be enforced, then the time has come to remove that law, or at least to change it substantially. The perception of much of the public is that the Shops Act 1950 is unenforced and unenforceable. But is this really so?

When the Auld Report asserts that the law "is widely disregarded by shopkeepers all over the country" (para 25), it presents no evidence in support of this claim. No surveys are cited because no data were collected. Doubtless, there are infringements of the law. However, the majority of these infringements are perpetrated by a relatively narrow section of the retail trade: DIY stores, furniture warehouses, garden centres, garage forecourt shops, small corner foodstores and illegal street markets. These infringements need to be put in perspective.

The Jubilee Centre is currently carrying out a survey across England and Wales to determine how widely infringed the law really is. So far, 42 surveys, carried out in cities, town centres and villages have been completed. The methodology has been to determine the centre of retailing activity and survey the entire area within a half-mile radius of this spot, between 10.00 am and 1.00 pm on a Sunday morning. The results are as follows:

Total number of shops in survey areas	11,731	
Total number of shops open	869	7.4%
Total number of shops in which:		
over 75% of estimated sales are illegal	92	0.8%
over 25% of estimated sales are illegal	161	1.4%

In other words, less than 8% of shops were open and out of these three quarters were complying almost entirely with the law.

It will be necessary to conduct surveys which take in out-of-town areas, where many of the small food stores, DIY centres and Sunday markets operate to get a more complete picture. However, to survey 11,731 shops and find that over 98% are complying with the law is highly significant. There is a great silent majority of shopkeepers who obey the law. Seen in this light, the National Consumer Council's remark, "there can be few laws which are more honoured in the breach"[49] has an air of unreality about it.

The Home Secretary puts forward this argument in a slightly different guise. It is not so much that the law "is being widely disregarded by shopkeepers all over the country". It is rather that "the law is being regularly, flagrantly and publicly flouted up and down the country".[50]

This is colourful language to use about some of the offences that are taking place. The general foodstore is frequently singled out as a common offender. A survey in Cardiff monitored the food and grocery purchasing behaviour of approximately 500 households over a six month period from January to July in 1982. Some 42.1% of Sunday purchases were of illegal products. This appears to be disregard for the law on a large scale until set alongside the other finding: "average Sunday expenditure across the 24 weeks accounted for less than one percent (0.96%) of total weekly expenditure ... 85% of trips made on Sunday involved expenditure of £2 or less . . ."[51] Offences on this modest, almost trivial, scale, do not constitute an argument for abolition of all restrictions. They suggest instead that the law might be brought into line with the *status quo* by adding an exemption for small, or independently owned, foodstores.

There are other offences which are more flagrant and public. The National Consumer Council were at pains to stress this. They commissioned a press-cutting agency to cut all press advertisements for Sunday opening in local newpapers from mid-October to mid-November 1983. They made a great deal of the fact that there were some 1,694 advertisements for shops opening illegally: "shopkeepers are not only breaking the law, they are spending money to advertise it too". In the words of the Auld Report. "the law is an ass" (para 28). It would be better to have no law than one like this which

---

[49] Evidence of the National Consumer Council to the Auld Committee, para 4.

[50] House of Commons, Official Report, 20 May 1985, Vol. 79, No. 120, Col. 750.

[51] N. Wrigley, C. Guy and R. Dunn, "Sunday and Late-Night Shopping in a British City: Evidence from the Cardiff Consumer Panel", *Area*, 1984, 16.3 pp 236-243.

brings the law into disrepute.

Blatant infringements of the law exist. The question once again is whether the nature and extent of these infringements justify the abolition of all restrictions on trading hours. This figure of 1,700 advertisements in one month needs to be put in perspective. In December 1984, there were registered with British Rates and Data some 1,218 weekly local newspapers, and 877 weekly 'free distribution' local newspapers. Adding these together gives a figure of 2,095 (which may be a slight overestimate or underestimate of the total number of local newspapers in England and Wales). We are therefore talking about less than one advertisement a month per newspaper in newspapers which carry scores of advertisements for retailers. What is more, some 1,247 of these advertisements for illegal Sunday trading, that is 74 per cent, came from furniture and DIY shops. In other words, it is not the retail trade, but one narrow section of the retail trade which is flagrantly breaking the law. Our survey result needs to be underlined. The silent majority of the retail trade is keeping the law.

These offences may be an argument for selective relaxation of the law. They are not an argument for its aboliton. However, it is not even clear that we have here a good argument for selective relaxation. We have a situation here which is analogous in some respects to terrorism. Those retailers who openly disregard the law may do so in part in order to bring pressure to bear on Parliament, not only by presenting their views, but by defying the law. In his speech to the Commons, the Home Secretary said:

"As a Minister whose primary responsibility is for law and order, I could not advise the House to let the present position remain unaltered".[52]

He might equally have said:

"As a Minister whose primary responsibility is for law and order, I could not advise the House to let itself be bullied into changing the law by every party or group so determined to get its own way that it is open in its defiance of the law. Such behaviour shows contempt for the law and by implication contempt for Parliament who made that law. It cannot be sensible to encourage attitudes and behaviour of this sort".

The issue is what constitutes a good argument for changing the law. In our view, the fact that a law is being broken is not sufficient on its own to justify its abolition. There need to be more positive reasons than this. The speed limit of 70 mph on motorways is frequently broken, and police will rarely attempt to apprehend someone who is exceeding the limit by only a few miles per hour. However, the law is kept intact because it does keep vehicle speeds lower than they would otherwise be, and by doing so reduces the number of serious road accidents, and saves lives. In other words, it is retained because it is sufficiently effective in influencing drivers' behaviour to secure its objective -

---

[52] House of Commons, Official Report, 20 May 1985, Vol. 79, No. 120, Col. 750.

the prevention of road accidents. Even the existing Shops Act, for all its weaknesses, is sufficiently effective to keep the vast majority of shops shut. In doing this, it secures a higher objective than precise enforcement of the law on trading hours. It keeps one day of the week largely free from commercial activity, releasing it for rest, recreation, worship and family togetherness.

There may well be a case for some selective relaxation of the law, but it must rest not so much on the fact that the current law is infringed by retailers, but on any positive grounds which may be found.

3. ENFORCEMENT BY LOCAL AUTHORITIES IS UNEVEN AND UNFAIR

Local authorities vary in the diligence with which they endeavour to enforce the law. A few authorities have determined not to enforce the law at all. Others select conspicuous offenders. By and large, authorities will only prosecute if they receive a specific complaint, rather than going out of their way to identify every offender. This produces inconsistency and injustice. Traders can often feel aggrieved because, when enforcement is less than wholehearted, some get away with breaking the law, and those who keep the law lose out.

The question is why enforcement is so uneven? Local authorities have a duty in law, under the Shops Act 1950 (Section 71) and subsequent edicts, to enforce the law. Nonetheless, many are reluctant to do so. Three reasons are suggested by the Auld Report. We need to decide whether they are reasons weighty enough to justify the abolition of restrictions.

One reason is that "even if a local authority does prosecute to conviction it knows that, in many cases, the small fines commonly imposed by magistrates will act as no deterrent at all to further breaches of the law by the shopkeepers concerned" (para 25). This sentence suggests that magistrates are themselves out of sympathy with the law and unwilling to make more than a token attempt to uphold it. There is something in this. The average level of fines in 1981 was £48.[53] However, we need to be certain of what they find irritating about the law. There is reason to believe it is the absurdity in the details of the law which have taken up of lot of court time over trivia rather than the broad principle of keeping Sunday largely free from commercial activity. In any case, the real problem is not magistrates, unwilling in this instance to do their duty of upholding the law, but inadequate levels of fines prescribed in law. The maximum penalty for breach of the Sunday trading regulation has only recently been raised to £1,000. There are many retailers who can swallow fines of this size as a cost to be deducted from profits. No wonder the "law is an ass". It has been given no teeth. Fines which are inadequately small are an argument for more substantial fines, not abolition of all fines.

[53] Evidence of the Christian Lawyers' Action Group to the Auld Committee, p. 4.

A second reason is that "the costs of enforcement at a time of severe financial constraint could be prohibitive" (para 25). This statement is highly suspect. When the Association of District Councils asked their 333 members to "specify expenditure incurred in 1982/83 . . . on enforcement of Shops Act [sic], they received 122 replies. The total expenditure was an average of £1,413 each. This is just over £27 a week, and could well be less than their budget for tea and coffee. On the other hand, enforcement does become expensive if prosecution fails to curb an offender. If the local authority is to continue to pursue its enforcement duty it must apply for a civil injunction under Section 222 of the Local Government Act 1972. This is costly in terms of legal fees, and can involve senior local government officers in time-consuming trips to London to see Counsel and to appear in court. This is not an argument for abolition of regulations, but for simpler procedures for enforcement if prosecution fails, either in terms of injunctions obtainable through a county court or through closure orders. To allow Sunday trading would be a strange way of reducing costs. It would require the supply of a number of municipal services on an extra day of the week. This is almost certain to raise expenditure, and hence rates.

The third reason that the Auld Report suggests for uneven enforcement is that the law is not popular - with traders or with the general public. A local authority will be reluctant to enforce a law which is unpopular with its ratepapers. We are in fact at the nub of the legal issues. Its importance merits a discussion under a separate heading.

4. RESTRICTIONS ARE UNACCEPTABLE BECAUSE THE PUBLIC NO LONGER APPROVE OF THEM

This is a major element in the Home Secretary's case. He argues that the current law "is unacceptable because it is no longer one that the majority of people want".[54]

At first sight, the majority of the public do want the law to permit Sunday trading. MORI has conducted surveys asking the question, "Do you think the law should be changed to allow shops to open on Sundays or not?" To take one fairly representative example, in the November 1983 poll, 65% said they thought the law should change in this way.[55] It is surveys like this one which are cited by those who say "the public want an end to restrictions".

It is often inappropriate to attach too much weight to the results of opinion polls. Surveys, in which a majority of respondents say they would like more shops to be open on Sundays, may reflect snap judgements which do not take

[54] ibid., col. 756.

[55] MORI, "Public Attitudes Towards Shop Opening Hours", November 1983. Cited in the Auld Report Appendix 6, Table E2, p. 193.

into account all the side effects. The attractions of freedom to shop seven days a week are simple to see. The disadvantages are not so immediately apparent. Some polls have tried to forestall this criticism by prompting second thoughts about the side effects. They have reminded people that prices may rise, or the noise might cause incovenience to them, but respondents have still been positive about Sunday trading. These questions, however, miss one of the main points, namely, that if I want to go shopping on Sunday, then I inconvenience *somebody else*.

It can also be argued that the public wants things which are mutually inconsistent. The public wants shops to be open because this would be convenient. At the same time, the National Consumer Council, in correspondence with the Auld Committee, say that "it is clear that there is a general desire that Sunday should be a 'different' day". In paragraph 66 of their evidence to the Committee, they note that "Respondents [to their surveys] felt very strongly that staff should not be forced to work on Sunday". There is a dilemma here, for it is not easy to see how we can have it both ways. The more Sunday trading there is, the more Sunday becomes a day like all the rest. The more Sunday trading there is, the harder it becomes to ensure that no worker is compelled to work on Sunday. Much as we would like to, we cannot have our cake and eat it.

Furthermore, it certainly cannot be said that they demonstrate a substantial proven demand for Sunday opening. The polls in favour of Sunday opening are difficult to square with the 1981 study by the National Consumer Council "into the problems that people face in doing their shopping [which] found that just one in ten respondents said they found existing shopping hours to be incovenient" (para 107). People may say that they think more shops should be open on Sunday, but when asked whether they would actually go and buy clothes and food in them, only 30 per cent said they would.[56] When this 30 per cent were asked, "How much money would you spend on food on Sundays if all shops were open seven days a week?", two-thirds of them said they would spend under £5.[57] In fact, "the goods which people suggest they would like to buy on Sundays are, in the main, those which are already available on Sundays" (Appx 6 para 8) which hardly suggests that the existing restrictions are particularly irksome.

Across only a narrow section of the retail trade can it be argued that this "substantial proven demand" exists. In a MORI Research Study, consumers were asked "if all shops were open seven days a week, including Sundays, which of these products do you think you personally would be likely to buy at least occasionally on Sunday?" For DIY/decorating materials, etc. and garden products, respondents replied 40% and 38% respectively. The next four types of goods suggested registered scores between 12% and 21%. The remaining twelve types of goods registered only single figure percentages.

[56] MORI Research Study conducted for the IFS, 1984. Cited in the Auld Report, Appx 6, Table 3.8, p.134.
[57] ibid., p. 196

The Auld Committee themselves concede that "it would be misleading . . . to leave the impression that there is an incessant general clamour for Sunday shopping or longer trading hours. Most people, even those who work full-time, do manage to buy what they need in the permitted times. Moreover, in general, working hours are becoming shorter, and if shop hours remain as they are now, people will have more, rather than less, time for shopping" (para 66). Furthermore, they will probably need to spend less time shopping since the increasing use of computers will make 'long distance' shopping by mail order or telephone easier, quicker and more attractive.

The argument that the majority of people are eager to end all restrictons simply does not bear close scrutiny.

5. IT IS INAPPROPRIATE TO USE THE CRIMINAL LAW TO RESTRICT TRADNG HOURS

This objection is raised on two differing grounds. The first is a concern that the criminal law should only be used to restrict trading hours if it can be ensured that the legislation will provide the basis for a good law. Otherwise the law will be brought into disrepute. A good law has certain features. The offence must be clearly defined, so that an individual can know whether he is engaging in an illegal activity or not, and the substance of the law and its penalties should be both acceptable and enforceable. Not all of our existing laws fulfil all these criteria by any means. It is a plain fact that some legal definitions are both vague and complicated, and that in some areas of the law enforcement rates are very low. Nonetheless, the laws are retained. We argue throughout this section that concern on grounds such as these produces a case for reform and some limited and selective relaxation of the Shops Act 1950, but not a case for wholesale aboliton.

The second form in which this objection is sometimes raised is that only activities which are a sufficient mischief should be incorporated in the criminal law. This can be a deceptive argument. When one uses the term 'criminal law', it conjures up to the layman images of major crimes such as murder and theft. The notion that opening a shop on Sunday should be treated in the same category sounds ridiculous to most people.

The criminal law, however, falls into two distinct branches. In the first, not only must it be proved that the defendant has committed the deed for which he is being prosecuted, but also some *mens rea* or 'mental element' on his part must also be proved. This part of the criminal law tends to deal with the offences which society considers particularly grave, and the 'mental element' can often, though not always, be concerned with motives.

In the second part of the criminal law, this 'mental element' is assumed to have existed, and all that must be proved is that the defendant actually committed acts constituting a crime. If he did, he is under a strict liability to bear the punishment for his crime. Offences of 'strict liability' form a large part of the criminal law and are often found where it would be difficult, if not impossible, to prove the existence or otherwise of a mental element. This branch of the law is concerned with a variety of trading and motoring offences. It is, for instance, a criminal offence for a butcher to display for sale bad meat; for a public house to be open outside licensing hours; for a driver to break a speed limit; or for a cyclist to cycle at night without working front and rear lights. It is under this part of the criminal law that restrictions on trading hours naturally fall.

If there were laws against trading on Sundays and they were not part of the criminal law, then they would be part of the civil law. Now, in a strict sense, the distinction between a crime and a civil wrong does *not* reside in the nature of the wrongful act itself. The distinction depends on a rather circular definition relating to the legal consequences which follow the act. A wrongful act which is capable of being followed by criminal proceedings is a crime; a wrongful act which is capable of being followed by civil proceedings is a civil wrong.

However, having said this, loosely speaking, crimes are deeds which in some sense are wrongs against society as a whole, whereas civil wrongs are wrongs against individuals (e.g. breach of contract, or defamation of character). The dividing line is necessarily hazy. However, it is clear that restrictions on trading hours could not be placed within the civil law. It can rarely be said that if a shop opens on a Sunday this is a wrong against a particular individual. However, if enough shops open on Sunday it has been argued this will be a wrong against society. If trading hours are restricted, these restrictions properly fall - indeed must fall - within the criminal law.

6. THERE IS NO VIABLE ALTERNATIVE TO TOTAL DEREGULATION

So far, this has been the trump card of those in favour of total deregulation. Even if some degree of regulation were desirable, no workable system of regulation is available. removal of restrictions is the only way forward.

This conclusion is based on the analysis of the Auld Committee, who examined the various suggestions which have been made for methods of regulation in Chapter Five of their Report. They consider a wide range including revision of the existing schedules of exempt goods, exemption by type of shop or by size of shop, exemption for self-employed retailers, an extension of present trading hours and the possibility of allowing local decisions. They reject all of them, however. The Home Secretary told the House of Commons: "the analysis is devastating. Each of the alternative limitations is shown to be either indefensible or unworkable".[59]

An examination of the analysis in fact suggests that the Committee's treatment of the subject was somewhat superficial in places and often noticeably one-sided. These weaknesses are readily apparent in the concluding paragraph of the chapter. The one-sidedness emerges when they say: "In our view, all the forms of control canvassed in our Inquiry,
while affording protection to some, would neglect the interests of others" (para 235).

They omit to mention the fact that their own recommendation neglects the interests of many - shopworkers, churchgoers, residents near shopping areas - while affording protection to none.

The Committee's analysis is also superficial. Each of the alternatives necessarily involves a complex discussion of issues, but each is dismissed after barely two pages of coverage. So the Committee concludes:

"More importantly, we are convinced that none of the suggestions for reform, short of complete abolition of restrictions, would work. None of them would work because they would not form the basis of a fair, simple and readily enforceable system of regulation" (para 235).

Now it is admirable to aim for a law which is fair, simple and readily enforceable, but it should be apparent that these three criteria are insufficient ingredients to ensure good legislation. Consider a hypothetical law: 'Everyone may do whatever he wants whenever he wants". This is fair - it treats everyone the same; it is certainly simple, and could not be easier to enforce. It would cause complete havoc.

Legislation has other objectives than enforceability and simplicity. However, as it pursues those objectives, such as the protection of valuable features or vulnerable members of society, there is usually a trade-off. Some of the enforceability and simplicity is lost. So, too, the fairness, since no law is equally good to all men. Realism tells us that any form of regulation of trading hours will lead to some untidiness, some unfairness in the law. It is a price that has to be paid.

One line or argument is that any form of regulation involves an arbitrary divide line between what is legal and illegal. By itself this objection is not compelling. The Government has set up over two dozen Enterprise Zones in which a range of tax burdens have been removed and a number of administrative tasks relaxed. At the limit this can give rise to a situation where one factory in the zone is paying no rates and another factory only 100 yards just outside the zone might be paying £20,000 a year. The boundary line is a sharp and arbitrary divide. But this is not used as an argument for extending tax relief and deregulation further and further. Nor is it used as an argument for doing away with Enterprise Zones, because their objective, the restoration of vigorous private-sector economic activity within the zone, is felt to justify and outweigh any injustices from the arbitrary dividing line which the policy

[59] House of Commons, Official Report, 20 May 1985, Vol. 79, No. 120, Col. 748.

involves.

In any case, the line drawn in Sunday trading legislation need not be particularly arbitrary. One possibility is to adjust the existing list of exempt goods in a piecemeal fashion, to remove anomalies (e.g. allow fish and chip shops as well as Chinese take-aways to sell fish and chips on Sundays) and to remove irrelevancies (eg. the exemption for partly boiled tripe). Then additions could be made, perhaps wherever substantial demand for the goods in question has been clearly demonstrated, which would imply allowing DIY and garden products to be sold on Sundays. The MORI Research Study carried out for the IFS confirms the existence of significant demand for these goods, at a different order of magnitude from demand for other goods. This option has attractions but one important objection to following this route is that it opens the door to an emphasis on the material wants of consumers involving a neglect of the human needs of shopworkers and others.

Some organisations have suggested that small shops should be protected. Their role in the community, in particular, the role of the small general foodstore in meeting the needs of pensioners and other disadvantaged groups has been noted. The problem is how to define 'small'. A possible solution would be to make the dividing line one based on the number of employees as there are precedents for this in other legislation in the field of Industrial Tribunals. Another possibility would be to allow independently owned shops to open since there is a qualitative difference between these and other kinds of shops. In other words, provided care is taken when regulation is developed, it does not have to be particularly arbitrary.

So far no alternative proposal has posed a serious challenge to the recommendation that restrictions be abolished. There are a variety of reasons for this. Some of the suggestions, such as exemption by type of shop or size of shop, could form the basis of legislation which would be quite as enforceable as much of our existing legislation. However, none has yet been fully developed and refined. The interest groups simply put forward suggestions because they assumed that the task of honing these down into legislative proposals belonged to the Government who have access to the relevant expertise.

Another problem has been that with so many alternatives about, some simply promoting sectional interests, the situation is analogous to one of "Divide and Rule". Those in favour of deregulation have had an easy job, picking off one by one the various suggestions for regulation. A serious challenge is only likely to emerge if those who wish to retain regulations unite behind some common proposal.

There *are* viable alternatives to deregulation. In Europe, Austria, Belgium, Denmark, Finland, West Germany, Greece, Ireland, the Netherlands, Norway and Switzerland, all prohibit or regulate Sunday trading by law (see Appendix). This is ample demonstration that it is perfectly possible to enact and enforce a law against Sunday trading. The issue is not one of legal feasibility, but one of political will.

7. THE IDEOLOGICAL ISSUES

For many people, the underlying issue is one of ideology. The basic objection to restrictions on trading hours is that they are restrictions. As the Home Secretary put it in the conclusion to his speech in favour of abolition:

"Many people want change for positive reasons - the main one . . [being] that restrictions on the freedom of traders to trade and customers to buy what they want, when they want, are inconsistent with the development of a free economy."[60]

The question, therefore, is how far it is right to pursue the development of a free economy. Free market philosophy tells us that if every individual seeks his own self interest, then the market's 'invisible hand' will bring about the best outcome for everybody. The majority of economists are agreed that in practice a free economy, based on the profit motive, is the best way of allocating scarce resources and encouraging initiative.

However, even on purely economic grounds, a totally free market does not guarantee the best outcome. The IFS conducted a survey of the relevant theoretical literature and concluded: "The fact that shops choose to open on Sundays does not guarantee that the gains derived from greater consumer choice will offset the additional costs elsewhere" (Appx 6 para 7). Retailers are prone to be trapped in what economists call 'The Prisoner's Dilemma', a form of market failure. The IFS notes that: "It might pay many individual retailers to open on Sundays even though it would pay all retailers collectively to shut on Sundays, and it is very likely that this is in fact the case" (Appx 6 para 86). As the John Lewis Partnership have pointed out: at a football stadium, the first person who stands up gets a better view, but soon everyone stands. The net result: no-one's view is improved, but everyone is standing instead of sitting. The first retailer who opens may gain, but in the end they almost all lose out.

A Christian critique of the free market would suggest two further weaknesses. The free market in the pure form has no built-in mechanism for ensuring a just distribution of the output it generates. Each individual enters the market place and attempts to secure the best return for himself by effective deployment of his labour and capital. However, some people begin with more capital or greater natural ability than others, and during the course of the market process some will be fortunate, but others will be unfortunate. In practice the free market tends to produce a polarisation of the rich and the poor. In the free market justice is purely concerned with protection of private property and ensuring that no breaches of contract occur. The biblical notion of justice, however, includes a persistent concern for the poor, and an

---

[60] House of Commons, Official Report, 20 May 1985, Vol 79, No. 120, col. 756.

emphatic rejection of any form of exploitation which might be inflicted by those with economic power on those without. This ideological discussion helps us to understand why the further development of a free economy in the direction of Sunday trading may give rise to exploitation of shopworkers.

The Achilles' heel of the free market, however, lies elsewhere. The market can only function efficiently if there are high standards of commercial honesty and morality. Initiative is only likely to be forthcoming in an environment where individual worth and individual responsibility are recognised and promoted. Both these conditions have existed in the West owing to the moral capital endowed by our Christian heritage. However, an untrammelled pursuit of the free market tends to undermine those conditions. In the Sunday trading context, pressure on family and religious life will weaken the two areas in which private morality is fostered. Taken to its logical conclusion, the free market erodes the very values required for its efficient functioning.

The argument in favour of removing restrictions is often based simply on the importance of freedom of choice, even if economic objections of this sort can be raised. This the philosophy of liberalism. It is an invigorating philosophy, picturing man as most himself when making choices. The more scope man has to make choices of his own, the richer his life will become. Our objective should be to maintain and extend individual freedom, where freedom is defined as a situation in which coercion of some individuals by others is reduced to the minimum possible degree. But here is the rub. Abolition of restrictions on trading hours causes a clash of freedoms.

There are different kinds of freedom: moral, intellectual, economic, social and political, but there may be competition in achieving freedom in these different areas. "Greater freedom in one realm of human action may make it either easier or harder to achieve freedom in another realm of action ... where there is a conflict of freedoms it is important to know it and to analyse their comparative value for the pursuit of happiness, present or future".[61]

This conflict of freedom can be seen in the abstract. A move to Sunday trading will place a premium on economic freedom at the expense of freedom of conscience and freedom to develop relationships with family and friends. The nature of the conflict is sharper than this, however. More freedom for some means less freedom for others. If consumers and traders are given unrestricted freedom to buy and sell, then the freedom of shopworkers and others to put their family or faith first is going to be seriously impaired. It is not just that some people will gain by the change and others will lose. It is rather that the *material wants* of some will be satisfied at the expense of the *human needs* of others. This is greed masquerading as a champion of freedom.

It is interesting to compare the Auld Committee with the Crathorne Committee of 1964 which also gave detailed consideration to the law relating to Sunday trading. They both begin from a premise which is designed to promote 'freedom', but the premise is very different in each case. The Auld

[61] F. Machlup, "Liberalism and the Choice of Freedoms" in E. Streissler (ed) *Roads to Freedom: Essays in Honour of Friedrich von Hayek*", Routledge & Kegan Paul, London, 1969.

74

Committee start from the premise that "the law should not interfere in the conduct of human affairs unless it serves a justifiable purpose or purposes in doing so" (para 29). The Crathorne Committee began from the general position that: "...the special character of Sunday ought to be preserved as far as practicable as a day of leisure in which a person is not required to pursue his weekday work and is free to do as he chooses" (para 17). Some have suggested that, as a compromise to maximise freedom, there should be deregulation of trading hours, but at the same time, to protect other freedoms, a statutory provision to make Sunday work voluntary. However, as we saw earlier, (see p. 52) this approach is full of pitfalls which almost guarantee that it will be ineffective.

Our discussion raises the question of what we understand to be the essential qualities of human nature. An ideology which over-emphasises the importance of the free market implicitly tends to represent man as no more than an agent of economic transactions. For the liberal, who emphasises freedom across a wider spectrum, "the essence of humanity lies in the capacity to choose".[62] Man is seen as most himself when making choices. The Christian can agree only so far. Man is most himself when he loves God with all his heart, and loves his neighbour as himself. We should do all we can to enlarge freedom of choice for people. Still more, however, we should do all we can to help human relationships in families and communities to prosper and flourish. Indeed a Christian conception of freedom attempts to synthesize the individual and the social aspects of freedom. "Human freedom is not freedom if it is not social; but neither is it freedom if it is not fully personal".[63]

All this raises questions about the basic function of the law. As we say, the Auld Committee start from the premise that the law should not interfere in the conduct of human affairs unless it serves a justifiable purpose or purposes in doing so. This sounds reasonable enough. However, because there is this presumption against legislation, the Auld Committee too readily latches on to an excuse, or difficulty, which permits them to argue that no such purpose exists. Their recommendation to end all restrictions owes more to their basic premise than to the evidence they consider. A more constructive way to look at the purpose of law is to argue that it should provide a framework within which all that is good for society is promoted, while all that is harmful is restrained (and if necessary punished). In this way, the law helps to strengthen the community. Where freedom is concerned exclusively in terms of the individual, a framework within which relationships are fostered will not usually be forthcoming. However, the fundamental flaw in minimising the role of law is that it rests on a naïvely optimistic view of man. If men are given *too* much freedom, particularly in the commercial sphere, there will always be a tendency for the strong to gain at the expense of the weak.

[62] C. K. Rowley and A. T. Peacock, *Welfare Economics - A Liberal Restatement*, Martin Robertson & Co. Ltd., 1975, p. 79.

[63] J. H. Olthius, "Self or Society: Is there a Choice?", Institute for Christian Studies, Toronto, December 1983

8.   CONCLUSION:
THE RESPONSIBILITY OF CHRISTIANS

During the course of his speech in the House of Commons, the Home Secretary said:

"I deeply regret and can readily understand the feelings of those who observe with sadness and regret the social changes that have taken place. But is it feasible for us now to turn the clock back?"[64]

This statement is almost calculated to mislead. The Home Secretary suggests that to keep restrictions on trading hours is to turn the clock back. No politician wants to be accused of that. What he conceals is what the Auld Committee themselves state:

"It would be misleading . . . to leave the impression that there is an incessant general clamour for Sunday shopping, or longer trading hours . . . Moreover, in general, working hours are becoming shorter, and if shop hours remain as they are now, people will have more, rather than less, time for shopping" (para 66).

In Britain, the special character of Sunday has been protected by regulation of trading hours for over five centuries. Against this backdrop, a decision to abolish all restrictions is irresponsible if it is unnecessary. It could be construed as a decision to manipulate the hands of the clock in a direction dictated by a faith commitment to the free market, regardless of the social damage that is caused.

The issue of Sunday trading is worth fighting about simply in order to preserve Sunday for worship, family and recreation. These are positive values in life which we should seek to promote. But there is more to it than this. The most alarming feature of deregulation of trading hours is the number of precedents that will be set. Disregard for the welfare of the church will be brought into the open. Family life will be placed under yet another pressure. The material wants of the prosperous and the profits of vocal corporate entities will have taken priority over the human needs of those with low incomes and little influence. A question of conscience will have been treated as party policy despite the misgivings of many MPs. A major social change, altering a longstanding characteristic of the British life, will have been introduced without having been mentioned in the manifesto of the political party responsible. Above all, Parliament will have visibly and symbolically rejected the notion that Christian principles should inform and influence legislation. Where is our society going?

This is not the place to attempt to answer in any detail the question of social involvement by Christians which has preoccupied so many in the church in recent years. We take as a point of departure what has been argued elsewhere,

[64] House of Commons, Official Report, 20 May 1985, Vol. 79, No. 120, col. 751.

most recently by John Stott in the book, "Issues Facing Christians Today".[65] This is a recognition that points of debate remain, but an appreciation that Christians, whether as individuals or in groups, should be concerned for society and active in trying to influence and improve it.

On an issue such as use of Sundays, many Christians are likely to feel that they should not try to impose their views on others. It would be narrow-minded, selfish and intolerant to do so. This is right. We should not *impose* our views on others. Christ does not impose his Lordship on anyone. In any case, to impose one's views will ultimately be ineffective as well. A country's laws must be built on consensus. No law will remain intact long if the majority cannot accept that it is a good law.

This does not mean, however, that we go to the opposite extreme and adopt an attitude of apathy or indifference to everything we see around us. We are to be concerned because God is concerned. "How can we acquiesce in things which passionately displease him, or affect nonchalance about a thing he is strongly committed to?"[66] In many Christians there is an unwillingness to express or commend the Christian view on society. We live an a pluralist society and need to respect people who hold different opinions from ours, or practise different customs. However, we do not press our views because they are ours, but because we believe that they are God's views too. In such circumstances, to be silent is to dishonour God. It is also a disservice to our fellow men, for we believe God's law to be for the good of man.

This leaves us with a better Christian response: we do all we can to "reason with people about the benefits of Christian morality, commending God's law to them by rational arguments".[67] To an extent, God's law is etched on to men's hearts, and they are capable of recognising what is good in it. Man has been given by God a mind, a conscience and the freedom to act as he pleases. In dialogue with anyone, therefore, we can hope, and often expect, to persuade his mind, touch his conscience and prompt him to action which will be more pleasing to God. Christians then should "seek to educate the public conscience to know and desire the will of God. The church should seek to be the conscience of the nation".[68]

Above all, the public needs to be convinced of the positive benefits of retaining Sunday as a day that is special, free from commercial activity. In an age which rushes us off our feet it affords an opportunity for rest and reflection; it provides time to strengthen and deepen relationships within the family and beyond it; and it lends itself to leisure and recreation of many varieties. The Puritans bequeathed much of immense value to the church in this country, but it is a legacy of the Puritan era along with some of the Victorian Sabbatarian societies that many in this country regard the Christian

---

[65] John Stott, *Issues Facing Christians Today*, Marshalls, Basingstoke, 1984.

[66] ibid., p. 50.

[67] ibid., p. 52.

[68] ibid., p. 51.

attitude towards Sunday as negative, restrictive and antiquated. Archbishop Coggan wrote in 1964: "We must work for conditions as will allow men and women not a Sunday which is dull and boring, but one which provides recreation of body, mind and spirit for refreshment and renewal of the whole person".[69] In the phrase of the Reverend Michael Sanders, "the Christian's witness to Sunday must essentially be postitive and life-affirming".[70]

Will all this 'persuasion' make any difference though? There are many today, Christians and non-Christians alike, who feel remote from the people and places where decisions are made. However, there is no historical warrant for this feeling that Christians can make no impact on society. History affords many examples of social progress through Christian influence. The Evangelical Revival of the eighteenth century "did more to transfigure the moral character of the general populace, than any other movement British history can record".[71] Neither is there any theological warrant. The Bible describes Christians as the salt of the earth. When salt was put on to meat, it would soak into that meat, and hinder decay. In the same way Christians should permeate and penetrate non-Christian society, and *can expect to hinder its moral decay*, provided they retain their distinctiveness as Christians.

It is encouraging to appreciate the influence that even a small minority can achieve, not just on one issue, but on a broad front. The remarks of Robert Bellah, an American sociologist, are worth quoting at some length:

"I think we should not underestimate the significance of the small group of people who have a new vision of a just and gentle world. In Japan a very small minority of Protestant Christians introduced ethics into politics, and had an impact beyond all proportion to their numbers. They were central in beginning the women's movement, labor unions, socialist parties, and virtually every reform movement. The quality of a culture may be changed when two percent of its people have a new vision".[72]

In recent decades, Christians have been slow to appreciate the significance of legislative changes which have chipped away some aspects of Christian morality, notably the relaxation of the laws on divorce and abortion. These have been part of a much larger process, one of fundamental change in the basic world view people have, away from a Judeo-Christian perspective towards a humanist-materialist one. The Sunday trading issue is perhaps an ideal opportunity to begin to reverse this trend. With its broad range of social implications, and its significance as a symbolic mark of Christian influence in legislation, it provides a rallying point for those who wish to begin to commend a thoroughly Christian view of man and society.

[69] Quoted in the Reverend Michael Sanders, "Sunday - a Day that is Different?", Research Project, St. George's House, Windsor Castle, p. 40.

[70] ibid., p. 40.

[71] J. Wesley Bready, *England: Before and After Wesley*, Hodder & Stoughton, 1939, p. 327. Quoted in Stott, 1984.

[72] Stott, 1984, p. 76. Taken from an interview with Sam Keen in *Psychology Today*, January 1976.

There is no reason to imagine that it is now impossible to prevent the arrival of widespread Sunday trading. However, if the battle is to be won, Christians need not only to be informed themselves, but to take every opportunity to alter the mood of public opinion, whether it be the views of the man in the street or the Member of Parliament. In general, there are many channels of communication which operate in society - letters to papers, articles in magazines, conversations with friends. However, there are certain strategic forms of communication which can often be particularly effective means of influencing opinion leaders and decision makers. The most obvious, and on this issue most effective, are visits and letters to MPs.

Over a number of recent issues, those with Christian sympathies have found themselves disturbed by a change in the law after it has been introduced. The opportunity to participate and influence those decisions was there but it was missed. This time, if we are to keep Sunday special, those with Christian sympathies must be sure to express their view clearly, effectively, and in time for it to be heard - which means now.

TRADING HOURS OVERSEAS

	Sunday trading?			Opening hours weekly	Saturday afternoons	Late nights
	Department stores super and hypermarkets variety chains	Large specialised businesses: DIY centres furniture warehouses etc	The law concerned			
Australia	No	No	Provincial	55-59	No[5]	Yes
Austria	No	No	Provincial	55-59	No	Yes
Belgium	No	No	558/71 passed 1973	44[4] 55-69	Yes	Yes
Denmark	No	No[3]	1976	45-49	No	Yes
Finland	No	No	1969	55-59	Yes	Yes
France	No[1]	Yes	Sunday rest (1906 and 1923) Code de Travail	55-59	Yes	Yes
Germany (W)	No	No[6]	Shop closing hours act 1956	55-59	Once a month and in December before Xmas	Yes
Luxembourg	Yes[2]	Yes	Arrèt grand ducale of 29.5.52	40-44	Yes	Yes
Netherlands	No	No	Winkelsluitingwet 1976	50-54	Yes	Yes
New Zealand	No	No	Federal law amended 1980		Yes	Yes
Norway	No[7]	No	April 1985	49-55	No	Yes
Sweden	Yes	Yes	Earlier laws abandoned after 1971	45-49	Yes	Yes
Switzerland	No	No	Provincial	45-49	Yes	Yes
UK	No (except Scotland)	No (except Scotland)	Shops Act 1950 Ch 28	45-49	Yes	Yes
US	Yes	Yes	Provincial (Blue laws)	50-54	Yes	Yes

Note: 1. In tourist areas some super and hypermarkets open. 2. All stores are allowed to trade until 13.00 on Sunday. 3. On the last Sunday before Christmas all stores open from 12 to 20 hours approximately. 4. According to a telex to the Retail Consortium in 1982 the law 558/71 of 1973 allows shops to trade for 44 hours in one week. 5. Saturday afternoon opening is starting in a few areas and was expected to grow in 1983. 6. Some furniture stores open on Sunday for prospective customers to look round (but not purchase). 7. A general prohibition against Sunday trading exists but may take place between 14.00 and 19.00 if authorities at the county level actively permit it.

General: In all the countries in this table there is a degee of legal Sunday opening which ranges from only newspaper stands, chemists and cake shops in Germany to the wide scale food trading carried on up to lunch time in France.

Sources for this table include:- Affärstiderna SOU 1977:72, Handelsdepartmentet, Stockholm 1977 - ILO, meeting of experts on relationship between hours of work and shop and bank opening hours, Geneva 1981 - In some cases information from different sources conflicts to such an extent that no entry has been made (eg. Canada).

This Table is reproduced by kind permission of the John Lewis Partnership who submitted it as part of their evidence to the Auld Committee. (See *The Gazette* 21 January 1984, p. 1173). It has been altered in respect of Norway where the law has changed since 1984.

COMMENTS

In all countries there is a degree of legal Sunday opening. However in the overwhelming majority of countries trading hours are regulated by law and Sunday is specified as a mandatory rest day.

Advocates of deregulation sometimes talk of the 'continental Sunday' with open shops and brisk trading. This is a misleading picture. Sweden in the only country in Europe which has no regulations on Sunday trading. Even the countries which adopt a relatively relaxed stance are a long way from total deregulation. In France, for example, before a shop may open on Sunday the standard procedure requires that agreement be reached between the employer, the employees and the Prefect of the district in question. In Luxembourg shops may open until 1 pm, but not in the afternoon, and this opening time is offset by the requirement that shops close on Monday morning. In Norway where the law was relaxed in April 1985 shops may only open in the afternoon, and only if the county authorities permit.

Meanwhile in Belgium, Finland, Greece, Ireland, West Germany, Switzerland, Austria, Denmark, and the Netherlands there is a general prohibition on Sunday trading. In the last three of these, shops must close not only on Sundays but on Saturday afternoons also. The same is true in West Germany for most Saturdays in the year. Thus in every country in Europe, except Sweden, there is some form of regulation of Sunday trading, a fact which never emerges in the Auld Report.

More often advocates of deregulation point to Sweden and Massachusetts, as evidence that deregulation has favourable consequences. This is a plausible argument. In Massachusetts where Sunday afternoon trading has been permitted since 1983, it is reported to be popular with retailers, shopworkers and consumers and the first six months saw an 18 per cent increase in retail sales (para 246). In Sweden where business hours have been unrestricted since 1972, there has been little upward pressure on prices, few problems over recruiting staff, and a boost to a new kind of retail outlet, the neighbourhood convenience store.

However in neither Sweden nor the U.S. has deregulation been an unmixed blessing. The experience of both countries clearly points to the erosion of Sunday as a day distinct from others. In the U.S., where Sunday opening began in the late 1950's, by 1982 some 77 per cent of independents and 86 per cent of chains opened on Sunday according to the John Lewis Partnership.[73] In Sweden, initially there was little Sunday opening, except by department stores which account for only 4 per cent of the retail sector. However when the IFS reported on a survey they carried out in 1984, they stated "... the picture that has emerged is that of considerable increase in the extent of Sunday opening ..." (Appx 6 Appx D para 13).

[73] *The Gazette* 21 January 1984 p. 1170.

For all this it is not clear that Sunday trading is a service which has proved necessary to consumers. In Sweden it is true that "30 per cent of households now shop regularly on Sundays with another 30 per cent doing so occasionally" (para 244). But the IFS "were informed that most shops closed at lunchtime on Saturday" (Appx 6 Appx D para 14). Thus over the whole weekend Swedish consumers do not have substantially greater shopping opportunities than consumers in England and Wales, where shops are open all day Saturday. For this reason the need to extend weekend shopping hours in England and Wales may be called into doubt, particularly if longer opening hours on Friday and Saturday evening were permitted.

Similarly in the U.S., although competitive pressures have led to seven day trading, in 1982 only five per cent of the week's customers did their shopping on Sundays.[74] The John Lewis Partnership see this as an illustration of their point that deregulation does not increase total turnover but it does increase opening hours and costs. They also argue that in the U.S. seven day trading has been one factor in the decline of the independent store and the increasing dominance of the multiple chains.

Even if an attractive picture of the economic effects of deregulation in Sweden and the U.S. is painted, two important notes of caution need to be sounded. First, it is simply the case that international comparison in retailing bristles with difficulties. There are important differences in terms of population density, female participation in the labour force, working hours, economic climate, the structure of the retail sector and the physical location of shops. The last of these can be particularly significant. Where shops are dispersed, whether because of the low population density or a pattern of shop location which is scattered rather than concentrated in the high street, shops which open put less pressure on other shops to open, and cause less environmental disruption. Both these favourable factors occur in Sweden and Massachusetts relative to England. In Sweden an exception to this generalisation might be Stockholm but there we find Sunday opening is much more prevalent than in the rest of the country (Appx 6 Appx D para 17).

The various ways in which countries and their retail sectors are different render any prediction based on overseas experience simplistic unless the differences are taken into account. But this is almost impossible to do with any accuracy. Even though must of the material on overseas experience of deregulation appears favourable to deregulation, and might have been used to bolster their case, the Auld Committee are unwilling to use it. "Our overriding conclusion from our review of the experience of other countries," they state, "is that their economic, social and historical traditions vary so much that none could provide a reliable guide for us. Comparisons with practice elsewhere are only of limited value in assessing what is likely to happen here" (para 248).

The other note of caution is to ask how far it would be wise to follow the

---

[74] *Progressive Grocer* April 1983. Cited by John Lewis Partnership in *The Gazette* 21 January 1984 p.1170.

practice of Sweden and the U.S. in any case. Both these are societies where the family unit has suffered even greater fragmentation than in Britain. Sweden is frequently noted for fluid, varied and casual relationships and in the U.S. the divorce rate is a staggering one in two and the median length of marriage a mere seven years. The direct link between the disintegration of family life and the deregulation of trading hours is limited (though Swedish union officials have commented that shopworkers find it difficult to arrange their family life). The indirect link is more important. They are both products of an ethos which places too much emphasis on individualism, materialism and economic freedom and too little emphasis on the other facets of human life, in particular the importance of human relationships. Once again the Sunday trading issue raises the question: "What kind of society do we want?"

BIBLIOGRAPHY

1. Association of Independent Retailers "Britain's Small Shopkeepers have given a Massive Thumbs Down to the Government's Suggestion of Unrestricted Trading" circular issued on 22 March 1985.

2. Beckwith R T and Stott W *This is the Day* Marshall Morgan and Scott, Basingstoke 1978.

3. Blomley N K "The Shops Act 1950: The Politics and the Policing" *Area* (1985) Vol 17 No 1).

4. Bowlby John *Child Care and the Growth of Love* Penguin 2nd edition 1965.

5. British Council of Churches and Free Church Federal Council "A Critique of the Auld Report" 1985.

6. Business Statistics Office *Business Monitor SDO 25 Retailing 1982* HMSO 1984.

7. Carson D A (ed) *From Sabbath to Lord's Day: A Biblical, Historical and Theological Investigation* The Zondervan Corporation Grand Rapids Michigan 1982.

8. Central Statistical Office *Social Trends No. 15* HMSO 1985.

9. Connor L J "Stopping Sunday Trading" *Justice of the Peace* Vol 148 No 39 29 September 1984.

10. Conquest Robert *Industrial Workers in the USSR* The Bodley Head Ltd. 1967.

11. Daws L F and Bruce A J *Shopping in Watford* Garston 1971.

12. Department of Environment, "Report of the Departmental Committee on Drinking and Driving" (The Blennerhassett Report) HMSO 1976.

13. Griffiths Brian *Morality and the Market Place* Hodder and Stoughton, 1982.

14. Harrison Jan "Attitudes to Bible, God, Church" Research Report The Bible Society June 1983.

15. HMSO The Shops Act 1950.

16. HMSO Shops (Early Closing Days) Act 1965.

17. Holgate G "The Extent of an Authority's Duty on Sunday Trading" *Justice of the Peace* Vol 148 No 48-49 1-8 December 1984.

18. Holgate G "Never on Sunday: Seven Day Trading" *Justice of the Peace* Vol 147 No 43 22-27 October 1983.

19. Holgate G "Video Hire Shops and the Shops Act 1950: A Postscript" *Justice of the Peace* Vol 148 No 18 5 May 1984.

20 Home Office "Report of the Departmental Committee on the Law on Sunday Observance" Chairman Lord Crathorne Cmnd 2528 HMSO December 1964.

21. Home Office "Report of the Committee of Inquiry into Proposals to Amend the Shops Acts" Chairman Mr Robin Auld QC Cmnd 9376 HMSO 1984.

22. House of Commons Official Report 20 May 1985 Vol 79 No 120.

23. Jaffer S M and Morris C N *Sunday Trading and Employment* Institute for Fiscal Studies 1985.

24. Johnston O R *Who Needs the Family?* Hodder and Stoughton 1979.

25. Kay J A Morris C N Jaffer S M Meadowcroft S A *Effects of Sunday Trading: The Regulation of Retail Trading Hours* Institute for Fiscal Studies 1984 (reproduced in the Auld Report).

26. Kirby D A "Shops Act 1950: Restrictions on Trading" *Area* (1984) Vol 16 No 3.

27. Latimer House "Sunday Trade - A Christian Perspective" 1985.

28. Lewis John Partnership evidence to the Auld Committee as reproduced in "Shop Trading Hours" *The Gazette* 21 January 1984.

29. Machlup F "Liberalism and the Choice of Freedoms" in E. Streissler (ed) *Roads to Freedom: Essays in Honour of Friedrich von Hayek* Routledge & Kegan Paul 1969.

30. Meza D de "The Fourth Commandment: Is It Pareto Efficient?" *The*

Economic Journal June 1984.

31. Market Opinion and Research International Ltd "Public Attitudes Towards Sunday Trading" Research Study conducted for National Consumer Council 1984.

32. Monopolies and Mergers Commission "Discounts to Retailers" HC 311 HMSO 1981.

33. Nash M L "The Law of Sunday Markets" *New Law Journal* Vol 134 No 6178 16 November 1984.

34. Olthius J H "Self or Society: Is There a Choice?" Institute for Christian Studies Toronto December 1983.

35. Robertson Elliott Faith "Professional and Family Conflicts in Hospital Medicine" *Social Sciences and Medicine* Vol 13A 1979.

36. Rowley C K and Peacock A T *Welfare Economics - A Liberal Restatement* Martin Robertson & Co. Ltd 1975.

37. Sanders Reverend Michael "Sunday - A Day that is Different" Research Project St. George's House Windsor Castle.

38. Schaeffer Francis A *A Christian Manifesto* Pickering and Inglis Ltd 1982.

39. Stott Reverend John *Issues Facing Christians Today* Marshalls 1984.

40. Study Commission on the Family *Families in the Future: A Policy Agenda for the '80s* 1983.

41. Tory Reform Group "Wages Councils" Discussion Document (unpublished) 29 April 1985.

42. Union of Shop, Distributive and Allied Workers "The Choice Must be Hours" Report on Shops Legislation 1984.

43. Wrigley N Guy C and Dunn R "Sunday and Late-Night Shopping in a British City: Evidence from the Cardiff Consumer Panel" *Area* (1984) Vol 16 No 3.

44. Young M and Wilmott P *The Symmetrical Family* Routledge and Kegan Paul 1973 Penguin Books 1975.

The views of the following organisations and individuals, and in almost every case their evidence to the Auld Committee, were examined:

Association of District Councils
Association of Independent Retailers
Association of Metropolitan Authorities
British Council of Churches
British Evangelical Council
British Hardware Federation
Church of England
Co-operative Union Ltd
Dr R L Davies and Mrs E Howard, University of Newcastle-on-Tyne
English Tourist Board
Evangelical Alliance
Free Church Federal Council
Free Presbyterian Church of Scotland
Dr Christina Fulop, City of London Polytechnic
Greater London Council
Habitat/Mothercare plc
Home Office
Horticultural Trades Association
Department of Trade and Industry
Institute of Shops, Health and Safety Acts Administration
Institution of Environmental Health Officers
John Lewis Partnership
Dr David Kirby, University of Wales
Lord's Day Observance Society
National Chamber of Trade
National Consumer Council
Retail Consortium
J Sainsbury plc
Scottish Office
Shaftesbury Project - Christian Lawyers' Action Group
Tesco Stores Ltd
Trades Union Congress
HM Treasury
Union of Shop, Distributive and Allied Workers
Woolworth Holdings plc
Workers' Christian Fellowship
Dr Neil Wrigley, University of Bristol

The Jubilee Centre
114 Barton Road
Cambridge, CB3 9LH

Tel: Cambridge (0223) 324606

THE JUBILEE CENTRE

Basis
To carry out research into contemporary economic and social issues in the light of biblical norms of politics and economics. The Centre is founded on the belief that the Bible is inspired in its entirety by God's Spirit through the human authors, and that it is the revelation of God. The name Jubilee Centre is derived from the Year of Release proclaimed every fiftieth year in Old Testament Israel, which was one of the main foundations on which Israel's social system was based. The aims are to propose policy alternatives to central government, the business community and the church on the basis of the research findings.

The Jubilee Trust is a charitable trust (Reg. No. 288783) and carries out research into biblical teaching on politics and economics.

The Jubilee Centre is a non-profit making trust and carries out research into areas of contemporary social policy, and encourages practical action by the Christian community on the basis of its research findings.

Council of Reference
The Rt. Hon. Viscount Brentford, Solicitor in London and Member of the House of Lords
Sir Frederick Catherwood, European MP for Cambridgeshire
Dr. Roy Clements, Pastor of Eden Baptist Church in Cambridge
Dr. Anthony Cramp, Director of Studies in Economics, Emmanuel College, Cambridge

Director: Michael Schluter, Ph.D.

Ways You Can Help
1. To read, discuss and comment on publications from the Centre.

2. To provide financial support for the research and projects the Centre undertakes.

3. If you are doing research yourself, to consider linking in your work in some way with the Jubilee Centre research projects.

JUBILEE CENTRE PAPERS
ALSO IN THE SERIES AND AVAILABLE SOON

Tick for
details

1. *Reconstructing the Extended Family:* ☐
   From Biblical Teaching to Public Policy in Britain
   This paper argues that the extended family, rather than the Western
   nuclear family, is the biblical pattern for family structure, and that it is
   vital that the political and economic system are designed to strengthen
   the family. After describing the biblical teaching, the paper examines the
   methodology for deriving principles and paradigms from biblical
   teaching and then applies the principles on the extended family briefly to
   four areas of social and economic policy in Britain today.

2. *Residential Mobility and Economic Policy* ☐
   The biblical teaching on land, roots and community is examined, and
   used to critique the contemporary emphasis on mobility in economic
   policy. Policies which might reduce levels of mobility are then discussed.

3. *The Christian Case for Family Associations* ☐
   This paper describes the mechanisms by which families disintegrate as
   economic development occurs. It then examines how family associations
   can help extended families stay together in the Third World, and help to
   strengthen what remains of them in the West. In the last section, the
   practical steps to setting up a family association are discussed.

4. *Israel: A Model for Church or State?* ☐
   Christians today spend little time studying Old Testament teaching. This
   paper seeks to answer the common objection that Israel's experience is
   only applicable to the church, and explores principles for applying Old
   Testament law and historical experience to contemporary nation-states.

From: Name ....

(BLOCK Address...

LETTERS .... Postcode...............

PLEASE) Tel. ....

Please send this page to: Jubilee Centre Publications Ltd.,
114 Barton Road,
Cambridge, CB3 9LH
England.
Tel. Cambridge (0223) 311596

NOTE: Any profits made on publications sold by Jubilee Centre Publications
Ltd. are used to finance further research projects by the Jubilee Centre.

DATE DUE

JAN 1 6 '91			